PENGUIN BOOKS

GREAT TALES FROM NEW ZEALAND HISTORY

Gordon McLauchlan was born in Dunedin and educated at
Wellington College and on various daily newspapers. That
training launched a career as a feature writer, magazine editor,
television presenter, radio broadcaster, social commentator,
historian, columnist and public relations consultant. His areas
of interest include literature, agriculture, tourism and media,
and he reckons he has worked in more branches of the media
than any other New Zealander. His books include *The
Passionless People* and *A Short History of New Zealand*.

GREAT TALES
from
NEW ZEALAND
HISTORY

Gordon McLauchlan

PENGUIN BOOKS

PENGUIN BOOKS
Published by the Penguin Group
Penguin Group (NZ), 67 Apollo Drive Rosedale,
North Shore 0632, New Zealand (a division of Pearson New Zealand Ltd)
Penguin Group (USA) Inc., 375 Hudson Street, New York,
New York 10014, USA
Penguin Group (Canada), 90 Eglinton Avenue East, Suite 700, Toronto,
Ontario, M4P 2Y3, Canada (a division of Pearson Penguin Canada Inc.)
Penguin Books Ltd, 80 Strand, London, WC2R 0RL, England
Penguin Ireland, 25 St Stephen's Green, Dublin 2, Ireland
(a division of Penguin Books Ltd)
Penguin Group (Australia), 250 Camberwell Road, Camberwell, Victoria
3124, Australia (a division of Pearson Australia Group Pty Ltd)
Penguin Books India Pvt Ltd, 11, Community Centre, Panchsheel Park,
New Delhi - 110 017, India
Penguin Books (South Africa) (Pty) Ltd, 24 Sturdee Avenue,
Rosebank, Johannesburg 2196, South Africa

Penguin Books Ltd, Registered Offices: 80 Strand, London, WC2R 0RL,
England

First published by Penguin Group (NZ), 2005
3 5 7 9 10 8 6 4

Copyright © Gordon McLauchlan, 2005

Designed by Mary Egan
Typeset by Egan Reid Ltd
Printed in Australia by McPherson's Printing Group

ISBN 978 0 1430 1963 3

A catalogue record for this book is available
from the National Library of New Zealand.

www.penguin.co.nz

CONTENTS

One

THE LEGEND THAT WON'T GO AWAY

Maori traditions say that Kupe was the explorer who discovered New Zealand, that he circumnavigated both islands, found them uninhabited and returned to his home, probably in the Society Group, with the navigational instructions on how to get here. That was some time in the tenth century AD. The story goes that it was 200 years or more before the next expedition arrived.

Kupe has been one of the most persistent heroes of Maori oral history, even though the legend in all its detail has been diminished decade by decade since it was the received word before the Second World War. Archaeologists, anthropologists and other scholars have gradually built up a picture of how and when New Zealand was discovered and settled and it doesn't leave any room for the romantic myth of Kupe. Or does it?

The story itself has major variations, depending on who told it and when. Joseph Banks, here with Captain Cook on the *Endeavour* in 1769–70, questioned some

Maori through the Tahitian interpreter, Tupaia, and was told Hawaiki was the original homeland and lay to the north in an area of many islands. Some Polynesians at the time of Cook, including Tupaia, seemed to have a rough map of the Pacific in their heads. But beyond that, not much information was sought or recorded.

The trouble is that by the time Pakeha sat down to methodically interview and transcribe the stories of Maori tohunga, who were the repositories of tradition, European sailors and settlers had been in contact for more than half a century, and a number of Maori men had been at sea on European ships. Just as the Bible quite quickly altered and confused Maori about their religion, social and political influences must have had a corrupting effect on Maori traditions.

The most assiduous recorders of Maori oral history were Elsdon Best and an English-born surveyor and eth-nologist, S Percy Smith, who died in New Plymouth in 1922, a year after the fourth edition of his book *Hawaiki: The Original Home of the Maori* was published. His work was done a century after first contact with Europeans but he was carefully listened to and his book widely read. In association with Maori elders, Smith used memorised genealogical tables to date reported events. Using these tables as his raw material, he wrote with great confi-dence on Polynesian history and claimed there were two Kupes, one in the tenth century and the second in the fourteenth.

'There can now be little doubt,' he wrote, 'that the first of the name was the real discoverer. He was one of those Polynesian navigators who had visited many of the islands, but whose home appears to have been Ra'iatea, of the Society Group. He was on a visit to Rarotonga when circumstances arose which started him on his voyage of discovery to the south-west. The reason why he took this particular course, like many other tales, partakes of the marvellous, whereas the true reason (as I believe) is that Kupe had observed on his many voyages the flight of the long-tailed cuckoo, year after year, always coming from the south-west and wintering in the Central Pacific Islands. He and his compeers would know at once that this was a land bird, and consequently that land must lie in the south-west.'

Another tradition – quoted by Smith rather dismissively as a footnote – is that Kupe saw in a dream the supreme god, Io, who told him how to find New Zealand.

John Palmer and Bernard Foster give another account of the discovery in the 1966 *Encyclopaedia of New Zealand*. They suggest Kupe killed the husband of a woman he coveted in Hawaiki and fled with her in the dead man's canoe, *Matahourua*, and 'in the course of their wanderings discovered New Zealand'. They say 'wanderings' because in 1966 some historians were in the grip of the drift theory that claimed Polynesians never really knew where they were going once they got far from home and found even the smallest distant atolls by accident.

Another version of the legend is that Kupe found New Zealand while in pursuit of a giant octopus, and that his wife, Hine-i-te-aparangi, gave Aotearoa its name after 'the long white cloud' that hovered over the new land.

While Smith referred to him as Kupe the Navigator, other accounts, including one written by Governor George Grey, suggest the navigator aboard the canoe was a man called Ngahue and that Kupe was the ranking chief. Most of the stories say Kupe arrived around North Cape, visited Wellington, sailed along the west coast of the South Island, gave many places the names they have today, and set out for home from the Hokianga.

Nothing of this can be corroborated by modern archaeological and anthropological research, which now offers a fairly clear picture of the process of Polynesian exploration of the Pacific. But when the expeditions first arrived is the most divisive issue among scholars. Over the years, the date for the first arrival of Polynesians in New Zealand has tended to get later rather than earlier, the thirteenth or fourteenth centuries rather than the tenth or eleventh. But, oddly, this fits in with Smith's genealogical count back to his Great Fleet theory – that the main body of Polynesian migrants arrived here en masse about AD 1350. But the likelihood of a number of canoes staying together over vast distances of the Pacific is remote.

However, Kupe is the legend that won't die. As the great Pacific scholar Peter Bellwood said, we should beware of dismissing traditions: they are not automatically wrong and undoubtedly contain some valid historical information.

A great leader called Kupe may well have existed at the time when the Polynesians were reaching across the Pacific and he may well have discovered New Zealand, gone back home and told his people of the very big islands to the south-west, given them sailing instructions, and thus passed into legend. Or he may have been the figment of a heroic people at a heroic time – the King Arthur of Maoridom. Either way, he belongs in the mythopoeic, outer region of New Zealand history.

Two

THE TIMID AND INCURIOUS TASMAN

History turned its back on Abel Janszoon Tasman because it decided he was too timid and too incurious to rank among the great explorers. There he was, on a fine summer's day, exultant you would think in the belief that he was on the western edge of Staete Landt (Staten Land), the great southern continent geographers had long ago decided existed to balance the huge land masses of the northern hemisphere. Even if it wasn't part of that continent it was, he decided, 'a very fine country'.

It was 19 December 1642. The previous afternoon, the two Dutch East India Company vessels *Heemskerck* and *Zeehaen* had moved warily into Taitapu (Golden Bay), Nelson. Two ship's boats out in front had made sure the water was deep enough. Tasman knew from fires along the shoreline they were being watched as they anchored about five kilometres from the beach.

In the dusk, two Maori canoes paddled out fearfully to look more closely at these floating visions, these ships so high in the water, with huge sails controlled by complex rigging, carrying pale men in strange clothes, aliens from a world beyond their experience, beyond their imagination. Even the small boats were paddled back to front.

The howl of Maori shell instruments, which sounded like 'Moorish trumpets' to the Dutch, was accompanied by unintelligible shouts from their 'strong, rough voices'. The shell blasts were no doubt to rebuff the spirits, challenge the invaders, and the rough voices a haka offering them war if they did not flee. The Dutch seemed to read these as gestures of friendship and replied with bugle blasts and loud calls of their own, adding to a stew of cultural confusion.

In the morning a canoe approached the ships and the Dutch displayed knives, linen and fish to encourage some Maori to come aboard and trade. They came close to the ships but the Dutch could make no sense of their shouts.

Tasman was the commander but the Dutch East India Company had a convention of leadership by committee, so the *Zeehaen*'s officers who were among the eleven members of the ships' council rowed over to the *Heemskerck* for a meeting, which decided the ships would sail further in towards the beach in search of a friendly association. While they were talking, seven more Maori canoes came out, each double-hulled and packed with up to seventeen stocky, yellow-brown men waving their paddles. The *Zeehaen*'s captain sent the cockboat back to tell his crewmen to be careful and not to let too many Maori on board. Emboldened, perhaps, by the passive response to their challenges, a Maori canoe hovering near the *Heemskerck* attacked. It rammed the cockboat at high speed, knocking the quartermaster overboard, and four sailors were dispatched with clubs. The canoe was then paddled for the shore with such 'unbelievable skill', according to the Dutch, that the occupants evaded fire from muskets and the *Heemskerck*'s guns.

Tasman and his officers were shocked far beyond what one would expect of worldly men in a violent time, men who had certainly killed 'Indians' in their time. Tasman's soberly written journal burst into flame at a 'villainous act' by 'these cursed men'. Following another council meeting, the officers resolved 'that the detestable deed of these natives that morning on four of the *Zeehaen*'s men should teach us to hold the inhabitants of this land as enemies'.

As more canoes came towards them, both ships fired, killing at least one Maori, but they refrained from more serious retribution. They sailed out of what they named Murderers' Bay, westwards out of Cook Strait (which they suspected was a strait but didn't bother to check) and up the west coast of the North Island, observing about a fifth of the New Zealand coastline before sailing off to the north.

The affair was enough to make Tasman and his men so timid about Maori they never set foot on land during their four and a half months off the coast. Certainly the booming breakers hitting the beaches gave them pause when twice they set out for land in search of water and fresh food, but over the weeks since Taitapu, they had built up Maori into giant bogeymen. Off Three Kings, they could see a small waterfall but also thirty or thirty-five men on the hills, exceptionally tall men who walked with 'enormous strides'. One sailor in the boat approaching the waterfall wrote: 'They came up to us, had wooden sticks about two fathoms or one and a half fathoms long and about two feet at the end; were very thick, as if they were clubs; they threw stones down upon us from above'.

To New Zealanders that's about all there is to Tasman – a timid man sent fleeing after one brief skirmish; and incurious. But his expedition was much more important than that and would probably have been accorded a higher place in history had he, like the later historians in this part of the world, been British. For one thing he was – albeit indirectly – responsible for the country's name. By 1648, Staete Landt had become Nova Zeelandia on copies of the chart made by Tasman's specialist pilot, Franz Jacobsen Visscher; it was named after the Netherlands' province, probably by Dutch cartographer WJ Blaeu.

One hundred and twenty years later, Tasman's story was almost obliterated by the brave, patient and inquisitive James Cook. Tasman had had the advantage of the magnetic compass and each decade since brought small but incremental advances in navigational techniques and technology. By the time of Cook's second voyage he had the chronometer, which at last made possible the accurate measurement of longitude.

And, anyway, Tasman was only nominally in charge. He was obliged to consult with a ships' council of senior officers and specialists, a cumbersome command structure that muffled decisive executive action.

In its time, the Dutch expedition was a bold venture. Tasman's countrymen had already charted the west coast of Australia and in 1627 had explored halfway across the south of the continent. He and Visscher had served the company on exploration and trading expeditions in the North Pacific and around the coasts of China and Japan. The company was not given to exploration for the sake of geographic knowledge; a drive to expand its interests through Tasman's expedition seems to have come from the Governor-General in Batavia, Anthony van Diemen.

So the two ships, both three-masted, the *Heemskerck* and *Zeehaen*, with a combined complement of 110, left Batavia (now Jakarta) on 14 August 1642 and sailed west. The *Heemskerck* carried nineteen officers and twenty soldiers, and the *Zeehaen* sixteen officers and eighteen soldiers. Twenty-one days later they arrived at Mauritius, a Dutch provisioning port for vessels sailing around the Cape of Good Hope between Holland and Batavia. They were, inexplicably, there for seven weeks. Tasman reported later that he received little help in reprovisioning his ships from the Dutch Governor of the Mauritius, while the Governor claimed in his report that Tasman spent most of his time wining and dining and would have been better employed supervising the work of his crew.

The expedition left Mauritius on 7 October. The route specified in the expedition's sailing orders, according to Dr BJ Slot of the General State Archives in the Hague, was a long way south. Had they persisted with their prescribed course they would have passed south of both Tasmania and New Zealand and sailed out into the huge empty region of the central South Pacific with nothing between them and South America. However, gale-force westerlies, low temperatures and poor visibility prompted Visscher to recommend a change of course to the north-east.

They found and charted the south coast of Tasmania on 24 November and named it Van Diemen's Land, then broke off to the east again. On 13 December, they saw 'land uplifted high' , the mountains of the South Island, from just north of Hokitika. The coast looked long enough to be the western edge of the fabled Staete Landt which had been drawn speculatively on some European maps. They cruised north and into the western end of Cook Strait towards their fateful meeting with Maori in Taitapu.

After they left New Zealand, the *Heemskerck* and *Zeehaen* rediscovered the Tongan group and sailed among the Fijian islands, before turning westwards for Batavia. Most important of all, they established that Australia was an island.

On Tasman's arrival back in Batavia, Van Diemen and his councillors proposed further exploration in search of gold and silver in the new southern region. They were rebuffed by the Netherlands office, which believed the company already had more than enough territory for trade. The new land was then neglected; one claim was that the Dutch kept their discoveries secret in case they were taken advantage of by rival maritime nations.

The Tasman mission was ultimately severely criticised because of the reluctance of its leadership to look into the economic potential of newly discovered lands and to search further east. It seems inexplicable now, as it did then, that Tasman and his officers did not try to find the southern limits of the South Island, or probe eastwards once they had cleared the north of the North Island. An epic journey in its time, it added incrementally to the knowledge of the Pacific but was, in the end, a failure.

THE TIMID AND INCURIOUS TASMAN

Abel Tasman's expedition unknowingly left two mysteries and a cultural gift for New Zealanders to contemplate. In Isaac Gilseman's famous drawing of Maori in Taitapu, no moko are shown nor any carving on the canoes, and the double-hulls are lashed together with no sign of the planks Tasman described in his journal. Is it likely these features would have escaped Gilseman's draughtsman's eye?

And the cultural gift is Allen Curnow's great poem *Landfall in Unknown Seas*, which was commissioned by the New Zealand government to commemorate the 1942 tercentennial of Tasman's visit.

Three

THE TRADERS OF KOHIKA

At Kohika, in wetlands near the coast on the Rangitaiki Plains, a chief lived with his family in a well-constructed whare richly decorated with carvings. The house was a metre above the lake, with canoes pulled up above the water's edge. He was the head of a small, affluent community of traders who had easy access by canoe to a transport network of interconnecting streams among small inland lakes, the Tarawera and Rangitaiki rivers, and the ocean. This gave the villagers great mobility.

Twenty-seven kilometres offshore was Tahua, a rich obsidian mine. The villagers not only used the stone to make their own tools, but the chief and his household also warehoused it and controlled much of the trade in obsidian from the coast to the interior North Island.

This was the late seventeenth century, 100 years before James Cook sailed along the coast of the Bay of Plenty on his first visit. The region, because of climate and fertility, had long been highly populated by Maori. Cook, who renamed Tahua as Mayor Island, also gave coastal Town Point its name because of the urban density of pa in that part of the Bay of Plenty – between the Maketu and Waihi estuaries – with the 'many fortified towns built on eminences near the sea along the shoreline', as he wrote in his journal. A large double-hulled canoe, capable of moving effortlessly among the offshore islands, hoisted a sail and ran alongside the *Endeavour*. As she drew close, her crew threw stones at the English ship until frightened off by gunfire.

A light but well-made palisade surrounded the pre-European Kohika settlement and on the nearby hills were fortified pa for security in times of regional political stress. The chief's whare was made of dressed planks and decorated with carvings. Alongside it on the lakefront were other houses, smaller, less well decorated, but with the same ready access to the water – a layout we would today call a marina. These other houses were substantial, but made of pole and thatch with facing boards carrying some lesser carved decoration. This was a hierarchical community. The chief was obviously an important man locally – but we will never know his name.

At least one of the storehouses built on poles also bore carvings. On slightly higher ground behind the line of whare were roofed storage pits, ovens and cooking shelters. The sandy soil and climate were just right for kumara. Fern-root was freely available around the settlement along with wild vegetables, including puha and marsh cress. Fish and seabirds were abundant. The villagers reared dogs, fed to fatness on fish and other food scraps of their masters. Flax was abundant and skilfully used, not only for clothing but also for fishing nets.

This was a well-fed, well-organised community which had reached a level of sophistication that allowed for the specialisation of labour and for sufficient leisure to encourage music, play, religious practices and the artistic decoration of artefacts and implements. And what an array of implements they had – dozens of gardening tools, bird spears, adzes, chisels, net gauges, and tools for rope-making and for twisting a fine, two-ply thread that may have been a local or regional invention. Among master carvers who worked there was one with an especially distinctive style.

Nature was munificent, but also capricious. Living at Kohika brought high rewards but the risks were great from floods and earthquakes. After one series of quakes, whare had to be rebuilt. Then a flood, a whiplash from the tail of a tropical cyclone, raced through the settlement, heaping silt in large new levees, destroying access to the transport network of waterways. Thus, after two generations of settled living, the villagers were forced to abandon their home.

Footnote: Artefacts were discovered in the peat and other sediments during the digging of agricultural drains at Lake Kohika in 1975. The Whakatane and District Historical Society found more by digging in the peat, and University of Auckland specialists have been involved in the archaeological work for some years, building a picture of the village and how it functioned.

Four

DALRYMPLE STRAIT?

In early 1768, Lieutenant James Cook was not the front runner to lead the British expedition into the Pacific that rediscovered New Zealand and put dozens of other island nations on the map. The Royal Society wanted the job to go to an ambitious Scot named Alexander Dalrymple.

Dalrymple was an accomplished man of twenty-eight when he returned to England in 1765 after working for the British East India Company since he was a teenager. He had travelled in India, China, the Philippines and other parts of South-East Asia. He had returned home on business, but a Royal Society plan to send an expedition into the South Pacific to observe the transit of Venus stirred a private passion. He was fascinated by the long-mooted possibility of a great southern continent. He wanted to go south. In 1767, to advance his claim to lead an expedition, he wrote and published *An account of the discoveries made in the South Pacifick Ocean previous to 1764.*

The main task for the Royal Society expedition was to

monitor the transit of Venus across the face of the sun from Tahiti, an island discovered only the year before by Captain Samuel Wallis in the *Dolphin*. The transit occurs only four times every 243 years and would predictably happen on 3 June 1769. The Royal Society planned observations from a number of sites, but it especially wanted one in the southern hemisphere because it would be visible in daylight only in that half of the world. Tahiti was, therefore, in the right place and, according to Wallis, likely to be sunny in June, the month in which he had arrived.

Why bother? The motive was purely scientific. Observations of differences in the transit's duration from various sites could provide data for calculating the diameter of the sun, and that would help establish the distance of the earth from the sun.

The Admiralty was to send the ship, and no one believed it would go all that way without afterwards having a serious look for the southern continent that cartographers had been drawing on the map for centuries on the grounds that some land mass would be needed to balance the continents in the northern hemisphere. This was Dalrymple's forte. The Royal Society advised the Admiralty late in 1767 that Alexander Dalrymple was their choice for taking command of the expedition because he had 'a particular Turn for Discoveries . . . being an able Navigator, and well skilled in Observation'. The terms were that he would go only as commander.

The recommendation lay around the Admiralty for a few months, during which time Dalrymple seemed the obvious choice. He had a say in the selection of the *Endeavour* as the right ship for the job – contrary to the long-held belief that Cook chose the ship because it had been a Yorkshire collier, the *Earl of Pembroke*. Not until April 1768, a few months before the planned departure, did the Lords of the Admiralty advise the society that the appointment of Dalrymple would be 'repugnant to the rule of the Navy'. Royal Navy ships could only be under the command of a naval officer. Whether from hubris or disappointment, Dalrymple confirmed he would go as the boss or not at all.

Forty-year-old Cook was an inspired choice by the Admiralty, but it was not without understanding his qualifications. The Yorkshireman, who worked as a farm labourer and then as an apprentice seaman on colliers before joining the Royal Navy, had displayed remarkable talent as a navigator and cartographer. What may not have been as obvious was the extraordinary strength of character that would make him one of history's greatest explorers.

Dalrymple is hardly remembered, although he was hydrographer to the East India Company and the Admiralty for more than forty years after being elected to the Royal Society at the height of Cook's fame, in 1771, as 'a Gentleman well versed in Mathematical and Geographical knowledge, & translator of Voyages to the South Seas & other places, from Spanish'.

Five

GOBLINS OR GODS – PAKEHA ARRIVE IN NEW ZEALAND

To pre-European Maori, their tribes were the separate nations of the known and visible world. Polynesians had been cut off from other races for at least two millennia before New Zealand was settled and Maori had been so long disconnected from their Polynesian homeland of Hawaiki its existence had become empyrean. The brief visit of Abel Tasman in 1642 had faded into the faintest myth in the South Island, if it was remembered at all, and no evidence is known of any other visit by a European ship.

So when the *Endeavour*, a squat, Whitby-class bark and former collier, sailed in close to the coast near where Gisborne is today, and strangely dressed beings disembarked into small boats, the effect on the locals must have been much the same as if a planeload of beings from a distant planet landed at Auckland International Airport.

In command of the *Endeavour* was a stocky, steady-nerved Yorkshireman, James Cook. He and his crew had known for several days, having seen seaweed and seabirds, that land was near, and several false sightings were made before twelve-year-old surgeon's boy Nicholas Young, from his watch in the crow's-nest, saw the certain shape of land emerge in the distance on the early afternoon of 6 October 1769. The *Endeavour*, coming from Tahiti, was sailing westwards in what Cook called 'gentle breezes and settled weather'. The sea coast was 'high with white steep cliffs [which Cook named Young Nicks Head] and back inland are very high mountains'.

The weather stayed clear as the ship went into the bay, sailing close enough to see people and houses on the shore against a backdrop of 'wood and verdure'. She anchored off the mouth of a small river.

Some aboard thought – as Abel Tasman had before them – that they were edging up to a part of Terra Australis Incognita, the great southern continent they were officially looking for. Or was it a large island? Cook was familiar with Alexander Dalrymple's *Account of the Discoveries made in the South Pacifick Ocean*, which included notes and drawings from Tasman's 1642 visit. Dalrymple was a believer in the southern continent theory. Cook kept an open mind. The Tahitian priest and navigator aboard the *Endeavour*, Tupaia, claimed to know from Tahitian lore of distant southern islands, but nothing of a continent.

Meanwhile, Maori, mystified and alarmed at something absolutely beyond their experience, watched the *Endeavour* approach. According to stories retold later, some thought it a sacred floating island with cloud-like sails pushing it towards them. Others thought it a great bird, its sails billowing wings. Were they goblins or gods? Maori were to ponder that over the coming days, these beings who paddled their boats backwards, who could kill birds and men alike from a distance with thunderbolts. Maori were very apprehensive but often stood their ground with courage that astonished the English.

On the afternoon of 8 October, Cook and his party ventured ashore in two of the ship's boats. For this first face-to-face meeting of Maori and Pakeha, Cook took with him the ship's surgeon William Monkhouse, Third Lieutenant John Gore, the gentlemen botanist Joseph Banks, naturalist Daniel Solander, astronomer Charles Green, and a party of marines (redcoats). On the beach, they left one boat in the charge of four boys and rowed the other across the river mouth, but the Maori they had seen there rapidly disappeared. Banks and Solander began collecting plants from the edge of the bush, but back at the first boat the boys were confronted by four armed warriors. Terrified, they tried to row the boat across the river but the warriors kept coming despite warning shots from muskets, and as one of them lunged forward with a spear, he was shot dead.

The next day, Cook and his party, heavily armed, landed on one side of the river, opposite a party of warriors drawn up on the other. An attempt to communicate with them triggered a fierce haka, so they pulled back a little until the marines had landed and were lined up in formation less than 200 metres behind them. Then Tupaia called out in Tahitian and, as Cook wrote in his journal: 'It was an agreeable surprise to us to find that they perfectly understood him. After some little conversation had passed one of them swam over to us, and after him, twenty or thirty more.' When the first man arrived unarmed, Cook handed his musket to an aide and the Maori and the English sea captain greeted each other, nose to nose, with a hongi.

When the others arrived, carrying their arms, Cook wrote: 'We made them, every one, presents but this did not satisfy them. They wanted every thing we had about us, particularly our arms, and made several attempts to snatch them out of our hands'. What had been a meeting became a mêlée. One warrior grabbed a sword and wouldn't give it up, encouraging even more aggressive behaviour from his companions. He was shot dead, and two others were wounded in the legs. The name of this second Maori to be killed by Cook's men was Te Rakau. According to Anne Salmond in *The Trial of the Cannibal Dog*, he was 'an important chief from the Rongowhakaata tribe, who according to local tradition had come with a party of warriors from Orakaiapu, a large fortified village in the south-west of the bay, to try to seize the *Endeavour*'.

When the warriors retreated, Cook formally declared the country a British possession and returned to the ship.

The following day, 10 October, Cook and his men rowed around the bay but could find nowhere to land because of the heavy surf. They came upon two canoes returning from a fishing expedition and decided to capture some of the occupants. Cook wrote in his journal, phlegmatically as always: 'Tupaia called to them to come alongside and we would not hurt them, but instead of doing this they endeavoured to get away, upon which I ordered a musket to be fired over their heads, thinking that this would make them either surrender or jump overboard. But here I was mistaken for they immediately . . . began to attack us. This obliged us to fire upon them and unfortunately two or three of them were killed, and one wounded, and three jumped overboard. These last we took up and brought on board (the *Endeavour)* where they were treated with all imaginable kindness; and to the surprise of everybody became at once as cheerful and as merry as if they had been with their own friends. They were all three young, the eldest not above twenty and the youngest about ten or twelve.'

The three Maori danced and sang and had conversations with Tupaia, who passed on information to Cook. They were given food and gifts and slept on board that night. They were reluctant to go ashore the next day but were placed on the beach.

Tupaia had been persuaded to join the expedition when it left Tahiti. He was of chiefly rank and defended his status, which he considered higher than that of the ordinary seamen aboard the *Endeavour*, and so he did not endear himself to the crew. Just how accurately he and Maori could converse is hard to gauge and remains a cause of argument. Certainly the two languages were closely related, although tonal and dialectal differences would have developed over several centuries of separation. More than one of those on the *Endeavour* noted that Maori spoke gutturally, which they must have meant in comparison with Tahitian.

Some further obfuscation would have attended Tupaia's efforts to translate Maori speech through Tahitian into English. Cook, Banks and others aboard had gained only a smattering of the local language during their long stay among the islanders. Tupaia, a clever and confident man, must have enhanced his halting English during the voyage, but language and cultural differences did cause irritations between him and those aboard the ship.

The *Endeavour* worked its way around New Zealand as Cook drew his remarkably accurate first chart of the coastline. Confrontations continued but Maori were now, like it or not, members of the wider world. Word of the strangers' presence spread rapidly, often well ahead of them, and both Cook and Maori leaders learnt much about how to relate to each other. He was surprised by their aggression, even after the lethal power of British weaponry had been displayed, and he and Banks were saddened by what they considered were unfortunate and unhappy killings and woundings.

Cook came back twice for extensive visits during the following decade. The second visit, in 1773, was in the course of a voyage (1772–75) to explore the South Atlantic and South Pacific, going as close to Antarctica as he could, in search of the elusive – and, as it turned out, non-existent – southern continent. The third expedition (1776–80) was in search of another fabled geographical feature – a shortcut north-west passage from the Atlantic to the Pacific.

Over the three voyages tension grew among the officers on how sternly Maori should be dealt with for pilfering or for taking goods offered for trade and absconding without payment. Some officers, like Gore, favoured harsh reprisals whereas Cook generally insisted on restraint. The great navigator established a reputation second to none in the annals of ocean exploration, and most historians would accept that his was a relatively humane and respectful introduction of European imperialism to the long-isolated Maori.

Footnote: Some confusion surrounded the exact date on which 'Young Nick' sighted the New Zealand coastline. Cook sailed the *Endeavour* south from Tahiti to 40 degrees, close to the latitude he knew Abel Tasman was on when he first saw the country from the west. Amid many false alarms from the crew staring into the west, unable to distinguish between land on the horizon and banks of clouds, Cook promised a gallon of rum and to name a geographical feature after the first person to make an accurate sighting of land. He is unequivocal in his journal about when that sighting was made: 'Saturday, 7th . . . At 2 p.m. saw land from the mast head bearing WBN, which we stood directly for, and could but just see it of [sic] the deck at sun set.' However, supernumerary Joseph Banks and others recorded that the 'Land Ahoy' call came in the early afternoon – but on 6 October, and Cook scholars have agreed. The explorers were working on English time, of course, well before the International Dateline was drawn down the globe but, even so, by 2 p.m. it would have been the same date here as in London. Cook was a precise man but on this occasion reckoned wrongly, by one day.

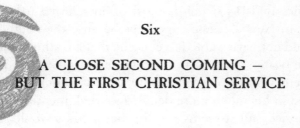

Six

A CLOSE SECOND COMING –
BUT THE FIRST CHRISTIAN SERVICE

From the mid-eighteenth century through the nineteenth, the French and the British were the main contenders for colonies in the South Pacific, and Jean de Surville was so close behind James Cook's rediscovery of New Zealand that they passed like ships in the night as they explored the coast, each unaware of the other's presence.

Cook arrived off Gisborne in the *Endeavour* on 6 October 1769, and on 12 December, Jean de Surville, in command of *St Jean Baptiste*, made landfall on the other side of the North Island, off Hokianga. About a week later, the ships passed within thirty kilometres of one another somewhere near North Cape. Cook named Doubtless Bay on 19 December because the wind did not allow his ship to enter the bay. A week later, better weather allowed de Surville to sail right in. He called it Lauriston Bay, but given Cook's persistent presence over the following decade, Doubtless easily won the nomenclature battle.

The French were in the vicinity over Christmas and it has been conjectured that de Surville would have had his Dominican chaplain, Reverend Father Paul Antoine Leonnard De Villeflex, say Mass on Christmas Day, either on shore or on the ship moored close by. This would have predated by forty years Marsden's Christian service in 1814 which is most often referred to as the first in New Zealand – perhaps because the Anglicans would not have wanted to concede that a Catholic might have beaten them to it. Neither de Surville in his brief log entry for the day, nor his First Lieutenant Guillaume Labe in his much more detailed journal, mentions such a service, but it seems certain that a Mass would have been said, given that a priest was among the ship's complement.

Comparisons between the two commanders can be gleaned from their logs. Cook was always in cool command, certainly on his first visit, and he prided himself on caring for the health of his crew. He also approached Maori with a surprising measure of respect, even if the early clashes did result in Maori death. De Surville was unquestionably a fine sailor. (At sea since the age of ten, he had worked for the French India Company, mostly in the Indian Ocean and around China; after serving in the French Navy, he went back to the Indian Ocean and was financed into an exploration of the Central and South Pacific.) He was an intelligent, fearless man, but seven of his men died from scurvy while the expedition was in New Zealand, and many were so sick when they arrived they took a long time to recover. He gave his sick crew members every consideration but clearly didn't understand scurvy and its causes as well as Cook did.

De Surville's descriptions of Maori are patronising. On his first venture ashore, he asked the local chief if he could fill barrels with water and noted that neither the 'feeble arms' or the 'poor fortifications' of the 'poor unfortunates' were 'capable of stopping us for a minute'. But for all his apparent arrogance, he had less trouble with Maori on first contact than Cook did. His behaviour was always polite: at one point in his log he says 'it is always better to begin relations with kindness and patience than by force and violence'.

Early on, he gave a Maori chief and some of his tribe who joined him on the ship a demonstration of cannon fire 'and they were all very frightened'. Then he presented the chief with a pair of pigs, trying to make him 'understand that by their copulation, if he kept them, he would get many more', which is perhaps understandable since pigs are mammals and New Zealand had none other than humans, dogs and bats. But he also gave them a cock and a hen with the same explanation. He must have thought Maori, who were surrounded by millions of birds, were very thick indeed.

His experiences with Maori were fine until New Year's Eve, when the ship's yawl broke loose and was spied on the shore. The French set off in the longboat but by the time they got to the beach, the yawl had disappeared. Maori had dragged it away and either hidden it among the dense reeds around a creek or moved it inland along the creek.

The next day de Surville wrote, 'I wanted to seek my revenge for the theft which had been carried out under our very noses and eyes.' With an armed shore party, he burnt many of the Maori houses and food storehouses and a canoe in the bay, kidnapped a Maori leader and took a 'beautiful canoe' aboard the *St Jean Baptiste*. His revenge would have had serious economic consequences for the locals.

He treated his Maori captive well enough, but the man died at sea of scurvy three months later. De Surville, too, failed to see the journey out. He was drowned in heavy surf while trying to land on the coast of Peru. His furious revenge at the theft of the yawl ended what had been a successful relationship with Maori and presaged the next French visit, by Marion du Fresne, two years later.

Du Fresne had also worked for the French India Company and served in the French Navy. One of his exploits was to rescue Bonnie Prince Charlie from Scotland after the disastrous defeat of the Scots at Culloden. In 1771, the French government provided him with two naval ships, the *Mascarin* and the *Marquis de Castries*, to explore the South Pacific. The ships arrived off Taranaki in March 1772, and reached the Bay of Islands six weeks later with both ships in need of repair after serious damage in a storm. The French stayed for five weeks, working on repairs, exploring the area and establishing a close relationship with local Maori, communicating by using a Tahitian vocabulary.

For a reason no one has established, the Maori invited du Fresne to a special ceremony on Moturua Island, where he had established one of two camps, and there he and his companions were murdered. The tally of French lives lost reached twenty-five after another group was attacked the following day. The visitors had to fight off further raids as they readied their ships for departure.

Then they took bloody reprisals, killing an estimated 250 Maori.

Although the expedition had taken formal possession of the country for the King and named it 'Southern France', its members departed in dismay, and the reputation of Maori as treacherous and violent discouraged the French for many years from considering New Zealand as a suitable country for colonisation. Although du Fresne's journal was lost, others in the party left accounts of Maori life that are among the richest of the early contact period.

A French expedition into the South Pacific in 1793 briefly touched on the north of the North Island with de Bruni d'Entrecasteaux in command of the *Recherche* and the *Espérance*. In 1824, the *Coquille* under the command of Louis Isidore Duperrey, with Dumont d'Urville second in command, spent two weeks in the Bay of Islands. Two years later, the last French expedition of exploration arrived in the *Astrolabe* (actually, the *Coquille* renamed), this time under the command of d'Urville, and spent three months complementing Cook's charts. A magnificent seaman and cartographer, and graceful writer, d'Urville added a huge amount of geographical, botanical and anthropological data to what was then known about New Zealand. Botany was a special interest, as was linguistics. He was a careful and useful observer of those parts of the country he touched. Of five volumes of his memoirs, published in the following decade, two were on his first two New Zealand visits.

He came a third time in 1840 in the course of a sweeping expedition to the Pacific, which included the polar regions. He spent a few days in Akaroa about the time the first French settlers arrived there. He later wrote of the visit, commenting on the Treaty of Waitangi and the British annexation. Only Cook contributed more to the early knowledge of this country. On his return to France, d'Urville was made a rear admiral; he and his wife and only son died in a railway accident near Versailles in 1842.

The British government showed little inclination to colonise New Zealand in the first third of the nineteenth century as French interest in the South Pacific increased. So when Jean Langlois, captain of a French whaler, reported back in France in 1838 that he had bought 12,000 hectares of land on Banks Peninsula, the Nantes-Bordelaise Company was formed. King Louise-Philippe agreed to provide transport for eighty settlers to make the journey to Akaroa. French warships were sent on ahead and the whole expedition caused a measure of panic among the British already living in New Zealand.

But by the time the French colonists arrived in 1840, Maori chiefs had signed the Treaty of Waitangi and ceded rights of sovereignty to Britain, and Governor William Hobson had arranged for the HMS *Britomart* to hurry to Banks Peninsula and hoist the Union Jack. The settlers stayed in Akaroa, however, and developed a charming and exotic town which became distinct from the surrounding quintessential English settlement of Canterbury.

The French continued to be a powerful force in the South Pacific, not only colonising the Society Islands and New Caledonia but, by their persistent presence in the region, forcing Britain to establish colonies in some places it had previously shown reluctance to control.

Seven

UTU AND THE *BOYD*

John Thompson, of the 508-tonne merchant sailing vessel *Boyd*, was a tough, experienced skipper not loath to use the despotic power available to nineteenth-century masters. Te Ara, son of a Whangaroa Maori chief, had served as a seaman on European ships for at least two years, long enough for him to speak English well and to have earned the nickname George. They came together in Sydney (Port Jackson then) in November 1809 when Te Ara and some other Maori signed on to work their way back to New Zealand on the *Boyd*. The result was a murderous hatred that led to New Zealand becoming a pariah nation, avoided for most of a decade because of reputed Maori savagery.

The *Boyd* had successfully carried a shipment of convicts from London to the penal colony of New South Wales, and the plan was to load ships' spars from New Zealand before returning home. According to varying contemporary accounts, all clouded by the extreme self-interest of witnesses, Te Ara decided that the work assigned to him on the ship by Thompson was beneath him; or he was ill and the skipper ruled he was malingering; or he was caught stealing.

Whatever the cause, Thompson had Te Ara tied to a mast and flogged, and his possessions taken from him. The young Maori still refused or was unable to work, so his food was stopped.

Thompson decided to seek his cargo from the shores of New Zealand's northernmost harbour, the Whangaroa. One claim is that he must have known this was Te Ara's tribal land because the Maori helped pilot him into the harbour entrance and to an anchorage off a nearby island. Once ashore, Te Ara told his brother, Te Puhi, and father, Piopio, of his treatment aboard the ship and the weals on his back and cuts and bruises on his arms would still have been fresh. Utu was inevitable.

The ship carried about seventy Europeans – the crew plus fifteen passengers on their way back to England. Passengers listed were Ann Morley and her new baby, Ann Glossop, Catherine Bourke, RW Wrather, James Moore, John Budden, John and Robert Thomas, Mordica Marks, John Petty, Thomas Martin, William Allen, William Mahoney and Denis Desmond.

A Tahitian called Jem, who had married into a local tribe, later reported that Te Puhi told Thompson he could guide him to the best kauri for spars and led the captain and his party into the bush. Without muskets, the Maori had to surprise the armed Europeans. They clubbed them all to death. Then they waited until dusk, returned to the *Boyd* in the ship's boats dressed in their victims' clothing, and killed everyone they could find. A few men escaped up the rigging and, when a neighbouring chief, Te Pahi, arrived in his canoe to trade with Te Puhi, they begged him to help them escape. He took them aboard his canoe and landed them ashore but they were stalked and killed. Many of the victims of the massacre were eaten by the tribe.

Once aboard the *Boyd*, the Maori searched the ship for muskets and gunpowder. According to a later account by Te Ara, his father tried to ignite a musket alongside a barrel of gunpowder brought from the hold, and triggered explosions and a fire that killed him and five others and burnt the ship to the waterline.

A few weeks later, the story of the massacre was relayed by a Maori to the supercargo (owners' representative) of the *City of Edinburgh*, Alexander Berry, as the ship loaded spars in the Bay of Islands. On New Year's Eve 1809, Berry, accompanied by a friendly Maori chief, Matenanga, set out with three boatloads of armed men for Whangaroa. They found the local Maori dressed in clothing they had taken from the people on the *Boyd*. Berry later reported: 'I inquired if there were any survivors, to which they readily replied in the affirmative . . . I then pointed to my men and their muskets on the one hand and to the heaps of axes on the other, bidding them take their choice. The chief replied that trading was better than fighting. "Give us the axes and you shall have the prisoners," he said . . .

'We were then told the prisoners were up country, that they would immediately send for them, and that they would be delivered up the next morning. At the time appointed, the natives . . . brought to our quarters a young woman with her suckling child, and a boy belonging to the vessel, about fifteen years old.'

The woman was Ann Morley. She had been found on the *Boyd* by an old Maori who had taken pity on her and her baby and held them prisoner. The boy was Thomas Davis, a crew apprentice, who was saved for one of two offered reasons: that he had a club foot which fascinated the Maori, or that he had offered succour to Te Ara during the voyage from Sydney.

Berry was also told that a little girl had been saved and he demanded her deliverance. After some negotiation, Betsy Broughton, daughter of the ship's commissary, was found enslaved by another chief on another, nearby island.

Ann Morley died at sea on her way back to England. Her baby and Betsy Broughton were then taken back to Australia. Davis went on to England but returned to Australia and drowned in an accident at the age of twenty-eight.

The *Boyd* massacre led almost immediately to another. A Captain Park of the English whaler *New Zealander* sailed to Whangaroa with a flotilla of whaling vessels and landed about 200 men. They killed Maori indiscriminately, burnt down their houses and destroyed their crops. The sad fact was they ravaged the land and people of Te Pahi, not Te Puhi.

The New Zealanders, as Maori were then universally known, already had a reputation for fierce savagery. Samuel Marsden, senior chaplain in the colony of New South Wales, was in London in 1808, persuading the Church Missionary Society to recruit and send back with him missionaries for New Zealand. He wrote: 'No clergyman, however, offered their services on this occasion. The character of the New Zealanders was considered more barbarous than that of any other savage nation, so that few would venture out to a country where they could anticipate nothing less than to be killed and eaten by the natives.'

After a time, two 'mechanics' were recruited: William Hall, a shipbuilder, and John King, a shoemaker and rope maker. They arrived in Sydney in February 1810 to receive what Marsden described as 'the melancholy news that the ship *Boyd* had been burnt and the captain and crew all murdered and eaten by the natives of Whangaroa. This most awful calamity extinguished at once all hope of introducing the Gospel into that country. Every voice was naturally raised against the natives, and against all who were in any way attached to their interest.'

He went on that 'another dreadful occurrence soon after took place', that the whalers, intent on revenge, 'landed on Te Pahi's island and there murdered every man and woman they could find. In this dreadful slaughter my friend Te Pahi received seven shots and died of his wounds. Many other friendly disposed people were killed.' An allegation by the whalers and others that Te Pahi was directly involved in the *Boyd* massacre was denied by Marsden, who said it was the similarity of the names Te Pahi and Te Puhi that caused the fatal mistake.

The effect of the *Boyd* massacre was immediate and resonant. The Church Missionary Society was intimidated and Marsden postponed the New Zealand mission project for five years. Early in 1814, Hall and another Christian 'mechanic', Thomas Kendall, made a visit to the Bay of Islands to appraise the situation. They reported back that they would take the risk of moving there with their families. Marsden agreed, sought and received a guarantee of protection from the Bay of Islands chiefs Ruatara and Hongi Hika and they all set out for Kororareka in the mission ship *Active* at the end of 1814.

On the way, the *Active* was held up by the weather off Whangaroa. Marsden decided he wanted to make peace with the chiefs there and put the *Boyd* affair to rest. Accompanied by Ruatara, Hongi Hika, Kendall, King, JL Nicholas (a friend of Marsden's and an aspiring writer) and others, heavily armed, they approached the Whangaroa chiefs. Te Ara, or George as Marsden always called him, claimed he had been sick when on the *Boyd* and had been brutally treated and abused by Thompson in terms, reported Marsden, 'which he mentioned and which are but too commonly used by British sailors'. Had that not happened, said Te Ara, the *Boyd* would not have been touched.

That night, Marsden, Hongi Hika and Nicholas slept in the camp among the local Maori and Marsden wrote later: 'Surrounded by cannibals, who had massacred and devoured our countrymen, I wondered much at the mysteries of Providence, and how these things could be. Never did I behold the blessed advantages of civilisation in a more grateful light than now. I did not sleep much during that night; my mind was too seriously occupied by the present scene and the new and strange ideas it naturally excited.

'About three o'clock in the morning, I arose and walked about the camp, surveying the different groups of natives; some of them put out their heads from under the top of their kakahu [flax mats], which are like a beehive, and spoke to me. When the morning light returned we beheld men, women and children asleep in all directions like the beasts of the field.'

Marsden was known as a harsh disciplinarian among his own people in Sydney, and yet he had a curiously sentimental attitude towards many Maori. His friendship with Ruatara, which began during a long association in Sydney, was important to him and he grieved deeply when the young chief died soon afterwards. He kept in touch with 'George' over the years and was satisfied the chief became contrite about his part in the *Boyd* affair. However, Nicholas later wrote: '. . . certainly the face of this man (Te Ara) bespoke him capable of committing so atrocious an act. His features were not unsightly, but they appeared to veil a dark and subtle malignity of intention, and the lurking treachery of a depraved heart was perfectly legible in every one of them.' Nicholas regarded the chief with 'abhorrence and disgust', adding: 'It was necessary, however, to be very circumspect towards this designing chief, and I took care that he should see nothing in my conduct that could lead him to suspect he was at all obnoxious to me.'

Eight

A SCENE DAUBED WITH COLOUR
AND LOUD WITH DEBATE

William Hobson was a small, prematurely aged, meticulous man, as strikingly different from a Maori fighting chief as a ceremonial sword is from a well-used patu, although he had previously been a fighting sailor for more than two decades. On 5 February 1840, he and his underlings put on the sort of pageant that the English, and especially the Royal Navy, were experienced and proficient at. What brought high drama to the occasion was the interplay between the sober, organised demeanour of the British and the spontaneous, dynamic response of the assembled Maori.

The eyewitness accounts of day one of the original, two-day Treaty of Waitangi gathering present a scene daubed with colour and loud with debate – a voluptuous picture of form and movement, genuine theatre, not without its comic asides. The sky was blue and the air hazy with summer as Maori from the region flowed in on that first morning by canoe or on foot. Lieutenant-

Governor William Hobson's ship, the man-of-war *Herald*, and other vessels were flying their colours. Along the side of a large marquee flew the flags of different nations which, as William Colenso wrote later, 'From the vividness of their colours, especially when the sun shone brightly on them, gave a charming air of liveliness . . .' to the scene.

The man who later laid out the plan for the city of Auckland, Felton Mathew, also described the colours and how they were picked out by the sun, and said he would never forget the scene until the day he died.

'Nearly in the midst [of the assembled Maori] stood Hakitara, a tall Native of the Rarawa Tribe,' wrote Colenso, that most literate of the observers. Hakitara was 'dressed in a very large and handsome silky white *kaitaka* mat (finest and best kind of garment, only worn by superior chiefs), fringed with a deep and dark-coloured woven border of a lozenge and zigzag pattern, the whole of Native (I might truly say of national) design and manufacture.

'The sunlight streaming down from an aperture in the top of the tent on this beautiful white dress threw the figure of this chief into very prominent and conspicuous relief, forming a fine contrast to the deep and dark shades of colour around; whilst here and there a taiaha, a chief's staff of rank, was seen erected, adorned with the long flowing white hair of the tails of the New Zealand dog and crimson cloth and red feathers.'

The Church of England missionaries may have been in black but the Catholic Bishop Pompallier was gorgeous, his gold chain and crucifix glistening on his deep purple habit. And it was this cast of clergy who provided some comic relief, with the Papist bishop upstaging the Protestants. Indeed, the occasion was so spectacular that the great Waikato chief Te Wherowhero, and probably some other leaders, refused to sign when the treaty was taken to them because they had heard of the pomp and ceremony at Waitangi and were offered no great show themselves.

The haste with which the day was organised made it surprising that it held so well together, especially in the face of powerful Maori suspicion and confrontation.

On his way to New Zealand, Hobson had stopped off in Sydney where Governor George Gipps formally placed New Zealand within the jurisdiction of New South Wales, swore Hobson in as Lieutenant-Governor and declared that land titles would be invalid unless acquired from the Crown or its appointees. This was because so many land purchases were being claimed, including huge tracts of the South Island.

Hobson set sail for the Bay of Islands on 18 January 1840, arrived eleven days later, and immediately arranged for the British Resident, James Busby, to organise a meeting of chiefs as soon as possible at Waitangi. Then Hobson set about organising the text. One of the reasons the British government wanted a treaty signed was because five years previously Busby had persuaded a number of northern chiefs to sign a Declaration of Independence, a move ratified at the time by the Crown and therefore given legal status. The new treaty was to allow the British government to change its mind, to legally undo that independence and, if you like, make both Maori and settlers colonial subjects.

Much goodwill towards the Maori existed in Britain

and among the missionaries. The treaty and the subsequent annexation of New Zealand were to protect Maori from the increasing number of European adventurers and settlers, and also from themselves. The first New Zealand Company settlers had already arrived in Wellington and set up their own little colony. Disputatious Maori tribes were unable and disinclined to impose a national rule of law among themselves. The riff-raff Europeans in Kororareka, and, more important, the growing number of land-hungry settlers throughout the country (including some missionaries) endangered the Maori future. Maori in turn were attracted to British goods and technology; and the Musket Wars had taken a terrible toll on some tribes and engendered war-weariness.

Hobson had notes of the Colonial Office's minimum demands but what he didn't have was legal expertise either from his own training or from his senior advisers. Also, he wasn't well, so Busby's later claim that he, not Hobson, wrote most of the English text is probably right. He certainly, significantly, inserted the clause that 'guarantees to the chiefs and tribes of New Zealand and to the respective families and individuals thereof the full exclusive and undisturbed possession of their Lands and Estates Forests Fisheries and other properties which they may collectively or individually possess so long as it is their wish and desire to retain the same in their possession . . .' Busby and Henry Williams insisted that Maori would not sign the document without a guarantee of that sort.

The whole process suffered from inordinate haste. Overnight on 4 February, Church Missionary Society veteran Henry Williams translated the document into

Maori with the help of Edward, his twenty-one-year-old son. So time for reflection on either the English or the Maori texts was limited; but at least the English version passed through a number of hands and heads, whereas the translated text suffered even more from lack of consultation on matters of fine meaning.

But the stage was set for the first meeting on 5 February as Maori walked or paddled to Waitangi from all directions to attend a party hosted by a man representing the most powerful monarch in the world. (Although at least one chief later would not sign a treaty of obeisance to a woman.) Hobson, in full dress uniform, stepped ashore around nine in the morning, walked to Busby's house, was assured by Williams and also Busby that the translated version of the text was accurate, and greeted a number of the local Europeans. Then, according to Colenso, Bishop Pompallier arrived and walked quickly, attended by a priest, into the reception room in which Hobson was holding court, brushing aside the uniformed police on guard.

'At this a buzz might be heard among the Natives,' wrote Colenso, 'one saying to another, "Ko Pikopo anakete hoa mo te Kawana" (He, indeed, is the chief gentleman! Pikopo [Pompallier] only is the company for the Governor).

'Hearing the observations made to the Natives, I repeated them to my brethren, Messrs King, Kemp, Clarke and Baker, at the same time calling their attention to what had just taken place, saying, "If Pikopo and his priest go in we, for the sake of our position among the Natives, should go in also".'

The brethren agreed but, as they approached the house,

an announcement was made that those who wished to be presented to Hobson should go in one door and out another. The Anglican missionaries realised that if they went in they would have to go out again while Pompallier remained inside alongside the Lieutenant-Governor.

When Hobson left the house to proceed to the marquee, Colenso reported that 'the Roman Catholic bishop and his priest stepped briskly up close to the heels of the Governor, so shutting us out unless we chose to walk behind them. "Brethren," I exclaimed, "this won't do: we must never consent to this position." "No," rejoined the Rev. R Taylor; "I'll never follow Rome."

'And on his so saying we stepped to one side out of the line of the procession.'

When they got to the marquee, Pompallier and his priest took possession of the seats immediately on the left of Busby, who was at Hobson's side, and left the Anglican clergy standing behind. The Colonial Secretary, Willoughby, took Colenso by the sleeve and said, 'Go over to that end and support your cloth.' Colenso wrote later that this was 'an intimation we lost no time in attending to, ranging ourselves as best we could behind the Rev. H Williams', who had seated himself on Hobson's right.

And so the resourceful, colourfully clothed Pompallier beautifully upstaged the men in black in what must have been, to the close observer, a small Trollopian farce. He had also, Maori reported later, tried to persuade them not to sign the treaty. And at a psychological moment on the following day, he extracted a promise of religious equality from Hobson.

The plan was that the treaty would be explained, its issues discussed, Maori would take a day to consider the treaty, and then come back and sign it two days later, on 7 February. Hobson, standing at the Union Jack-draped table on the platform, spoke to the 200 or so Maori crowded inside the marquee, with Williams translating, urging them to sign the treaty to provide the Queen with the authority to control the Europeans settling in the country and protect Maori rights and property. After Hobson's coolly persuasive introductory speech, he read the text in English and Williams read the Maori version.

What followed was a disheartening parade of Maori dissent as chief after chief warned against signing the treaty, prancing and gesticulating as they spoke. Several told the Lieutenant-Governor to go home, or casti-gated the missionaries for taking their land. One chief, Te Kemara of Ngatikawa, ran forward and thrust his finger at Williams, shouting, 'You, you bald-headed man, you have taken all my land.' In a debate that dragged through the long hot day, only a few chiefs spoke in favour of the treaty, most notably Tamati Waka Nene, the Hokianga leader who was then and remained a firm ally of the British.

Overnight, Maori became restless and some left for home early the next morning as the food ran low. The missionaries worried that more would follow, leaving the treaty unsigned. Hobson, called unexpectedly, hurried to the marquee in civvies with only his uniform hat. Both the English and Maori texts were read again and Hobson refused further argument and insisted he would only take signatures.

Hone Heke was invited to sign and, as he stepped up to do so, Colenso sought assurance that the chiefs fully appreciated what they were putting their names to. He expressed his concern that Maori would later be angry if they thought the missionaries had persuaded them to sign up to something they imperfectly understood. Heke signed, followed by forty-four others, mostly with drawings of their moko. Copies of the treaty were then taken around the country for signing by local chiefs, although some of the major tribes – notably Waikato and Arawa – never did.

This was the apogee of Hobson's career. The Irishman, who joined the Royal Navy as a ten-year-old, served it in the East Indies, West Indies, the North Sea, and the Mediterranean for nearly thirty years. He had an excellent reputation: enhanced by his commodore at the West Indies station who referred to him as 'an officer who to the most persevering zeal unites discretion and sound judgement'. However, had Hobson served a full term as Governor it is likely he would have failed. It became apparent early that he thought governing settlers would be the same as commanding a ship, with orders meeting an orderly and unreserved response. It made him unpopular early, as the Royal Navy background helped make Robert FitzRoy bitterly unpopular after him.

Nine

ELIZA'S LOVE AFFAIR – ONE AMONG FEW

Eliza Hobson, wife of New Zealand's second governor, was a gentle woman who seemingly charmed everyone whose life touched hers and was the object of her husband William's frequently professed ardent love.

William Hobson, who signed the treaty of Waitangi on behalf of Queen Victoria, a man not known for his eloquence or easy affections, wrote from Sydney to Eliza in London on the occasion of their ninth wedding anniversary: '. . . this blessed day, nine years since we were united, not in form merely but in truth. Our sympathies, our loves and our wants, and nine years of the tenderest affection have cemented our union in bonds of natural confidence. What greater blessing can man look for on earth.

'When this reaches you the term of our separation will be reduced under a year, and with God's blessing it is to be hoped we will be in the enjoyment of each other's society within this period. Then indeed will our situation be enviable. How eagerly I look forward to it.'

The lovely Eliza Hobson was the warm heart of perhaps the only deeply passionate love story recorded among early Pakeha New Zealanders, conventionally within marriage though their passion was. Grand passions so effulgently romantic that they burst from the constraints of convention and titillate the public imagination – Lord Nelson and Lady Hamilton, for example – are conspicuously absent from our history. And no haughty mistresses, no courtesans, sparkle in the New Zealand story.

In a strikingly appropriate way, our puritanical society produced only one outstanding woman absorbed in the inexorability of sexual attraction – Ettie Rout, a practical, sensible Kiwi whose preoccupation was contraception to prevent the spread of disease. No single gallant blithely strides across the history of our social life; no alluring, eloquent Don Juan or Lord Byron to fill the dreams of New Zealand women living their sexual lives vicariously.

Our great love stories come from Maori legends of such impassioned women as Hinemoa and Pania of the Reef. Hinemoa's lover, Tutanekai, lived on Mokoia Island in Lake Rotorua and nightly played his pipe to attract Hinemoa from her village on the shore. Her people hid or guarded all their canoes to prevent her from joining her lover, of whom they disapproved; so she swam to the island and into his arms. Pania, a mermaid who lived beyond a reef just off the shore of Napier, fell in love with a young chief, Karitoki, but was compelled to return to her people of the sea. A bronze statue in the city enshrines her unfulfilled yearning to be reunited with her lover. But in the context of Victorian mores, the love affair between Eliza and William Hobson shines as intense, sincere and enduring.

They met in Nassau in the Bahamas, in the mid-1820s, soon after he had been promoted to Commander aboard vessels operating against pirates and slave-runners. Eliza Elliott was sixteen, the only daughter of a Scots West Indian merchant, when they were married at the end of 1827. He was thirty-four. Six months later he was paid off and the couple moved to Plymouth. It wasn't until the end of 1834 that Hobson got another job, as Commander of HMS *Rattlesnake*, the ship that was to take him to Australia and New Zealand. Two daughters and a son were born while the couple were together in Plymouth.

While he was away in the southern Pacific they wrote frequently. 'My dearest Liz,' said a letter in 1836, 'Your letter and the accounts I have received of you so completely fill me with joy . . . Rest assured, my treasure, that my greatest consolation since I left home has been derived from the Knowledge that you are placed beyond the reach of want . . .' Perhaps unusually for their time, he consulted her and sought her approval for any big decisions, any career move he might make. When he wrote that he might be appointed Governor of New Zealand, he added, 'but . . . I will not stir an inch without your full concurrence'.

He returned to England on the *Rattlesnake* and when he sailed again for New South Wales in August 1839 to be sworn in as Lieutenant-Governor of New Zealand, a pregnant Eliza and their children accompanied him. Not long before they arrived in Sydney, their fourth child, Emma, was born. The family stayed behind when

Hobson proceeded to New Zealand, later joining him in Auckland.

While Hobson was stiff and formal in his official capacity, he melted before Eliza and she before him. It seemed to their colleagues and friends that this awkward man was a more amiable and hospitable person in her company. Wrote Felton Mathew, the surveyor who set out the plan for the new city of Auckland: 'There is an excellent trait in Hobson. He is so fond of his wife and family and so desirous of having them with him.' And at a vice-regal function she was praised for her 'kindness, urbanity and hospitality' which drew the 'respect and esteem from all who had the honour of knowing her'.

Hobson was promoted to Governor of the new colony of New Zealand after the Treaty of Waitangi was signed, but his tenure of office was brief. He was tested by conflict with the leaders of the New Zealand Company settlement in Wellington and when he had to visit the town aboard the brig *Victoria*, he wanted his wife to accompany him. However, she had to decline, although lamenting, 'I cannot bear to think of his going for they have treated him so ill. They deserve nothing at his hands'. She was pregnant with their fifth child and feared seasickness.

The Wellington settlers did indeed treat him ill again, intolerant as they were of any contradiction of their assessments of how the colony should be run. But they wouldn't have much longer to castigate him.

While in the West Indies gaining the light of his life, he had been infected by the blight of it – yellow fever. He suffered two serious bouts of the fever and his health thereafter was always fragile, leaving him often fatigued, sometimes too sick to work, and suffering from persistent headaches. He had suffered a stroke soon after his arrival in New Zealand and in September 1842 a second killed him. His beloved Eliza and their children were bereft. Even those who had opposed Hobson politically could not bring themselves to hold back from praise of her. Indeed, his obituaries more often than not gave space to praise for her gentle benevolence.

So a genuine New Zealand love story came to a sad, premature end. Eliza and her family stayed on for most of a year before they returned to England. She was expansively farewelled from Auckland, the occasion for many friends to regret her going. She left with many gifts and much well-wishing, amid some really bad poetry, such as:

> *Playful we've seen thee smiling*
> *Within the festive hall*
> *Unwittingly beguiling*
> *The yielding hearts of all.*
>
> *We've seen thy gentle bearing*
> *Thy offices of love*
> *We've heard thy voice endearing*
> *Like an Angel's from above.*

She never returned to New Zealand and, despite her youth, beauty and charm, never remarried. She died in 1876.

Ten

FEAR CAME LIKE A COLD FOG

Hone Heke was a central figure in New Zealand's early history, a man so assertive and with so much mana among Maori and Pakeha he gave his name the power of myth by repeatedly cutting down the flagstaff above Kororareka, defying the settlers and standing up to the government and British soldiers. He was baptised by the Reverend Henry Williams, educated at the Church Missionary Society school in Paihia, was the first chief to sign the Treaty of Waitangi, and then, as the dominant figure in what became known as the 'War in the North', gave British authority its first serious challenge.

One claim is that the first American consul in New Zealand, the English-born trader, James Clendon, encouraged Heke to read Thomas Paine's *Rights of Man*. No Maori leader had, before this, directly and with an organised force confronted Pakeha settlers since the signing of the Treaty of Waitangi.

It was equally true that Maori had never gone to war

on any scale against British troops. If Frederick Maning is to be believed in his book *War in the North*: 'Great, indeed, was the fear of the Maori when they heard of these soldiers, for all the Pakeha agreed in saying that they would attack anyone their chief ordered them to attack, no matter whether there was any just cause or not; that they would fight furiously till the last man was killed, and that nothing could make them run away.'

Maning assumed the persona of 'an old chief of the Ngapuhi Tribe' in writing the story. He continued: 'Fear came like a cold fog on all the Ngapuhi, and no chief but Heke had any courage left.'

A nephew of Hongi Hika, Heke was six feet tall and powerfully built, an established Ngapuhi warrior by his early twenties. At first, he saw advantages in the Pakeha presence in Kororareka, the populous first capital which serviced the hundreds of whaling ships operating in the South Pacific. He had also sold land in the north and at one time levied a toll on travellers as they passed through his base in Kaikohe.

Then Governor Hobson moved his capital to Auckland on the Waitemata Harbour and most of the maritime-servicing business followed him. The introduction of customs duties at all ports forced up prices, and levies from shipping now went to the government. As the Northland economy became severely depressed, Heke saw his influence and opportunities for revenue sharply decline. He also sensed that Maori independence was being usurped by Pakeha, a belief reinforced by the action of government ally Waka Nene and other chiefs, in handing over a young Maori murderer, Maketu Waretotara, to the British authorities for trial in Auckland (see next chapter). Heke wanted Maketu dealt with by Maori.

So, for all these reasons, he reacted by cutting down the local symbol of British authority – the flagpole on Signal Hill above Kororareka – on 8 July 1844. It was an act of nuisance to Pakeha. But when he repeated the attack on 10 January the following year, Governor FitzRoy sensed insurrection and sent to New South Wales for more troops. He offered £100 for Heke's capture. The flagstaff was re-erected immediately but a week later the defiant Heke cut it down again.

The next flagstaff was sheathed with iron, a manned blockhouse was built beside it, and both were surrounded by a palisade. The 400 or so people in the town below began preparations to defend themselves when they heard that Heke and fellow chief Kawiti were gathering warriors.

Kawiti feinted with an attack to the south of Kororareka at dawn on 11 March. The detachment in the blockhouse raced outside to assess the scale of the attack and Heke and some of his men occupied it and, yes, destroyed the flagstaff for the fourth time.

Women, children and non-combatants were evacuated to ships anchored in the bay. The fight for the town was a stalemate after some fighting with losses on both sides when, about one o'clock in the afternoon, an ammunition store under the house of Joseph Polack spectacularly blew up. This seemed to unnerve the defenders, who abandoned the town altogether, protected by a bombardment from ships in the bay. All the Europeans fled to Auckland with stories of an imminent Maori uprising that sparked an alert in the new capital.

Left without opposition, Heke and Kawiti's men sacked Kororareka, stripping what they wanted and burning all the buildings – except for missionary property, including the church, which still stands, with bullet holes testimony to the battle that briefly surged around it. Frederick Maning suggested that the Maori burnt the town because the ships in the bay were bombarding them.

The War in the North continued with British troops sent from Auckland by the strong-minded new Governor, George Grey. But Heke and Kawiti inflicted a humiliating defeat on the British regulars at Ohaeawai before retreating for a last stand in a new pa at Ruapekapeka. British artillery ensured a victory, and Heke and Kawiti surrendered – but not abjectly. Indeed, Heke was brazen enough to suggest that if peace was to be agreed then the Governor should go to him and seek it because he wouldn't go to the Governor. To everyone's surprise, Grey did approach the chief to arrange peace. According to Maning's character, this made Heke 'the greatest man in this island . . . All the Europeans are afraid of him, and give him everything he asks for, for if they refuse he takes it, and no one dare say anything to him.'

But the young warrior's body was weakened by his battle wounds. He died in 1850, aged about forty, and was given a Christian burial. He had proved two things that were to have an impact on the history of the next two decades. One was that Maori could face British troops with confidence in their own bravery and military cunning; and the other was that defensive pa such as the one that he and Kawiti built at Ohaeawai were an excellent way of frustrating and even defeating the British.

The War in the North was over after the battle for Ruapekapeka. The next and much graver threat to the future came with the New Zealand Wars in the 1860s.

Eleven

MAKETU AND THE DEATH PENALTY

Maori in the Bay of Islands were baffled and then morally offended by the ponderous nature of British justice when the government charged a Maori teenager, Maketu Waretotara, with murder at the end of 1841, the first capital charge since authority was vested in the Crown following the Treaty of Waitangi. The well-connected Maketu seemed incapable of telling lies but apparently had inherited a murderous rage. He was working on the farm of Elizabeth Roberton on Motuarohia in the Bay of Islands when a fellow employee, Thomas Bull, abused him once too often. Maketu killed him.

Mrs Roberton was the widow of a sea captain-turned-farmer who had drowned off the island early in 1840. She had decided to stay and manage the farm with hired help. According to his own story – and he continued to candidly incriminate himself even at the formal inquest – Maketu went to Mrs Roberton after killing Bull and told her what had happened. She abused him too, so he killed her, her infant daughter and Isabella Brind, a small half-Maori child in her care. He chased her seven-year-old son to the top of a nearby hill and flung him over a cliff, then returned to the Robertons' homestead and set fire to it. Two men from Kororareka went to the island to investigate the smoke and found the grisly scene.

Angry Europeans in the town insisted the murderer be dealt with. However, the local magistrate had two police officers and no soldiers to confront dozens of Ngapuhi who quickly gathered on Motuarohia. Maketu was the son of a Waimate rangatira, Ruhe, and was related to Pomare and other leading Northland chiefs. Local Europeans became alarmed that an uprising was imminent.

Missionary Henry Williams arranged a hui at the Paihia mission. According to Maori lore (tikanga), Maketu's killing of Bull was justified under the principle of revenge, or repayment (utu), but the half-Maori girl was the granddaughter of another rangatira, Rewa, and was Rewa not entitled to utu? The hui resolved to send a letter to Governor Hobson saying that they regretted the teenager's killings, that he acted alone, and they had no intention of rising up against the Europeans. The letter was signed by powerful rangatira – including Maketu's father – and he was handed over for trial.

Among the dissenters was the irrepressible Hone Heke, who argued that Maketu should be dealt with in the Maori way, and that by handing him over to Europeans they were abjectly conceding the right to govern their own affairs; and it was true that the settlers were very pleased to consider the case as an acceptance by Maori of British justice. Williams said afterwards that had it not been for the killing of Rewa's granddaughter, the likelihood of their handing over Maketu would have been seriously diminished.

With the arrival not long beforehand of the first Chief Justice, William Martin, and the first Attorney-General, William Swainson, the structure for a major criminal trial was in place, and the settlers hoped the showcase of justice would impress Maori. The crime was committed in November 1841, the trial held in Auckland, and the execution on 7 March 1842.

However, Maori thought it cruel that someone who had confessed repeatedly that he was guilty should have to go through a long trial with a defence lawyer making what was to them an incomprehensible case. They could not understand why a man who had confessed and was to be executed was not immediately killed with a swift blow to the head in a humane and honourable way. And when Maketu was found guilty and condemned to death, they considered it callous and stupid that he should be held for a week where he could hear carpenters building a gallows on which to hang him.

The Reverend Churton was assigned to achieve the baptism and repentance of the young Maori whose age was uncertain but was certainly not more than eighteen. Maori must have been further mystified when Maketu signed a statement on the morning of the hanging that read: '. . . it is right that I should die, it is my own doing, and for my sins I am going to the place that is burning with everlasting fire. If I don't repent my sins, but I have prayed to God to wash my sins away with the blood of Jesus Christ.' He then forgave all concerned.

A church service to pray for his soul was attended by

leading citizens, including Governor and Mrs Hobson. Many more, though, in fact hundreds, attended the public hanging.

Footnote: Motuarohia is now more commonly known as Roberton Island.

Twelve

THE DIARY OF WILLIAM DAWSON Esq.
SHOPKEEPER, WELLINGTON

A few days after my tenth birthday my father looked into my face with a sudden intensity, as though he'd noticed me at last, as we sat at the table about to eat dinner in the middle of a Sunday, and he said: 'I've signed you up for an apprenticeship. You're going to sea as a boy.'

What did I think about that then? He said it rather than asked it.

I did not know what I thought about it because I did not understand the import of it. He had always just told us what was happening to us. All of us. Mother too. He knew how to manage a family because he would say he did, and because we had the evidence. My mother was setting the dinner on the table this day, as he spoke – meat, potatoes and bread it usually was at Sunday dinner – and we were warmly clothed and the fire was burning in the parlour as well as the kitchen where we ate. Mother nodded approvingly as my father patted my arm and touched my head in what for him was a powerful excess of emotion and said: 'The company will make something of you. You are a good enough boy but you do not have the patience for my business.'

My sisters, Jessie who was fifteen, Mary who was twelve, Glenda eleven, and my brother James who would have been five at that time just sat there slack-jawed staring at me.

'Not right away,' Jessie blurted out. 'When father?'

'Hush girl.' My father had a way of clenching his jaw after each sentence and pausing for a few seconds as though worried something he might be sorry for would escape, or as if he wanted to be as parsimonious with words as he was with money. What with this and his always slightly bowed head, he seemed under siege to a hard life and could only talk about serious things in small doses.

My mother took him as seriously as he wanted to be taken, complimenting him on his wisdom and even thanking him on our behalf. 'William is so grateful,' she said as though I was some kind of figment. 'You have been so good to all your children.' But he sat still, hunched over, looking at the table, not acknowledging the flattery, his mouth tight as though all the clenching had made it impossible for him to smile. He might have been thinking of a next sentence but he said no more until the next morning as he set out for work. 'I will take you down to docks tomorrow morning to meet Captain James Grant as runs the Star Line,' he said. Then: 'Have his clothes packed, Mrs Dawson, in a canvas bag.'

I remember this scene so clearly because what I did understand immediately was that it was the end of my childhood, so I mulled it over a lot. My family has always since been just a memory blurred around the edges of this very clear picture of one Sunday dinner.

My father was chief bookkeeper with William Barnaby and Son, Shipbuilders, and had been since it was just William Barnaby, Shipbuilder. The job allowed him to rent a tiny cottage in as respectable an area as possible in which he could still be close enough to the docks where he worked. But he was a fragile man with bronchitis that wracked him whereas I was made after my mother's family with a wide chest and strong legs. My father was tortured by a sense of obligation towards his family and was wanting to get us all settled before some final calamity struck his thin body. He had taught us all to read and write competently and Jessie and I were the two who enjoyed learning most and were best at it, Jessie at reading and me the quickest at arithmetic. So, although he was mean with the small things of life, I remember him as a kindly man who wanted the best for us but did not flaunt his kindness.

And remember him from those days I must because I never set eyes on him again after that Tuesday morning when I met Captain Grant and then Captain William Cudgeon pushed me up the gangplank onto a creaking old leaky ship they called the *Challenge*. I am not sure whether Captain Cudgeon ever saw me again either for that matter. I waited on him hand and foot all the way to Sydney Town and even though he occasionally cuffed me on the side of the head when I was late with his supper, he never spoke just growled. As I say, I do not know that he ever actually saw me, William Dawson, or just another brat.

The rest of the crew bullied me, and worse, and for the

THE DIARY OF WILLIAM DAWSON Esq

first few weeks after we left England I was fearful all the
time and would try not to think about my lot in this whole
new world, except that sometimes I would pull the rough
grey blanket over my head and sob all the worry and fear
out of me. The Mate, Jed Buckett, said one morning, 'I
will tell you something William Dawson: there is nothing
wrong with a boy or a man crying when the world gets
on top of him but if it gets a hold of yer, if it's the thing
yer do most of the time, then it will rot your soul just
like the salt water and the worm rots this old tub.'

I have since seen the rot in other boys and the better
their previous life, the harder it was for them to rise away
from their fear and sorrow. Some of the worst deserted
in foreign ports and God knows what happened to them
then. I cannot say Mr Buckett was kind to me but he was
not unkind either. He was a Christian and did not see us
as people so much as sinners and took upon himself the
task of reforming the scoundrels in the crew. Waste of
time it was, keeping on and on and on at me and anyone
else who had to listen about the drink and lust and how
they made men devils. But a Mate is the one who sets
the tone of a ship and so it was a happier ship than some
of them with rum-sodden beasts as Mates. The captain
was distant but the Mate was one of us. Mr Buckett
made me attend to the provendoring lists and when
he was convinced I could do my sums right, he got me
navigating and all kinds of what he called brain work. My
handwriting was flowing in the way a bookkeeper's is so
I mostly wrote the ship's log with someone at my elbow.
That's how I got to be a Mate, but that's later.

When I think back to my childhood Jessie comes into
my mind more than my mother who I remember as Mrs

Dawson. Jessie brought me up even though she must have been a little girl herself when I was born. She was the one who dressed me and fed me from as early as I can remember and she is the one who cried inconsolably that morning when I walked out the door with my father. I cannot quite remember my mother except as a bundle of clothes bustling around the kitchen. Jessie and I still write, more often now than we did for many years. The third time the *Challenge* arrived in London from Sydney Town I took the train to Southampton where she lived with her husband, a carpenter in the Royal Navy. I still have great affection for her but I stopped pining for her after that. I have not been back to the old country for seven years now and it is of no great concern that I probably never will now. Except it would be nice enough to see Jessie again, an old woman now, and her kids and their kids.

'Them's New Zealanders,' Charley said quietly when he saw me jerk my head around in surprise as we walked into the door of the bar in Sydney Town.

'God Almighty,' I murmured under my breath.

'Take no notice. They been here for near to a week waiting for a vessel to take them home. They got dumped here by a whaler for some trouble or other.'

They were half lying half sitting against the back wall. One of them was eating potatoes and meat and what looked like cornmash and milk, and the other was abstractedly smoking a pipe. Neither of them seemed to have noticed us. Staring ahead, they were, at nothing, but with that feral look of extreme alertness and fear in their eyes that were framed by the whorls of their tattoos.

'They go quiet, inside 'emselves when they have got nowt to do and are not among their own,' Charley said later after some sailors came in and the noise built up and the palpable tension created by the New Zealanders was swamped by the noise. I had been thinking about going to New Zealand and trying for some land. For three years now I had been Mate on an old tub, the *Bristol*, working between Port Jackson and Port Phillip and sometimes Adelaide. I had been prudent, had kept away from the grog, so had a bit of money. Maybe enough even to buy a piece of land which is what everyone who had any money aimed for.

'The talk is all about New Zealand,' I said to Charley as we walked back to the ship. 'About a healthy climate like the old country, only better they reckon, and if you do not get in before the place becomes a colony you will not get cheap land. But then they reckon the New Zealanders are dangerous and those two back there looked pretty fearsome to me.' One of them had gone out to the lava-tory at the back of the bar and though he wasn't much taller than me he was massive around the shoulders and had that kind of shuffle men get when their thighs are muscled up.

'They will not be when it becomes a Colony. They'll send the soldiers in.' Charley was changing his tune. He had worked the whalers for a few years and had been to Kororareka and to a sealing station on the west coast of the big Middle Island and used to tell me about the *Boyd*, a ship the New Zealanders burned in 1809 after killing everyone on board, men, women and babies. The New Zealanders liked fighting just for the hell of it, he used to say. I reminded him of that.

'The Royal Navy will take a couple of regiments in and that will fix it.'

'Well why don't you go over?'

'I might at that. The trouble is the New Zealanders will not be peaceful until after it is a Colony, although the missionaries seem to have calmed them down, they say.'

Charley told me about Kororareka and about mission stations in the north of the country. They were like little colonies on their own, very isolated and had to depend on the local Maoris or supplies from Sydney Town. Small colonies were being set up in the Middle Island where there were few Maoris and wide grasslands. If only he had the money, Charlie said, he would buy land down there but he was too old now. Companies formed in England were planning to send out settlers by the shipload and a shrewd man would get in at the beginning.

I wasn't old though. Twenty-nine, ten years younger than the century I was, and I decided I wanted to see New Zealand for myself. My chance came when the owner of the *Bristol* who sold her to some fool in Port Phillip paid me off. Without too much thought, I grabbed a berth on a sealer and we headed for the west coast of the Middle Island. Any job on shore would be better than that, though. I was cold and wet all the time and clubbing and spearing seals and paring back the blubber was a miserable and stinking way to earn a living so I begged to be paid off and even took less than I was owed to get off at Kororareka near the top of the North Island, and away from its drunken master.

I got the odd job on the wharf and did some carpentry but within two years I decided I would have a quick look down south where the New Zealand Company had settlements called Wellington and Nelson, and then I would head back to Port Jackson and go back to the sea.

It was a woman who did for me. In Wellington. I married her and took over her father's shop at Karori. It was easier than a Mate's work. I never did go back to England and now that Jessie's dead, there's no one there I think about at all.

From Memoirs of an Early Settler *by William Dawson.*

Thirteen

THE PERFECT BUSHMAN BRINGS BRUNNER BACK

After sixteen months in the remote West Coast bush, Thomas Brunner awoke one morning to find one side of his body paralysed. Rain had been pouring down for weeks and winter was not far away. Later that day, as he lay there wet, cold and unable to move, he was mortified to hear one of his Maori guides, Epiki, trying to persuade the other, Ekehu, that they should leave him there to die. Epiki said that Brunner was too ill to recover and there was no food near where they were camped. Epiki and his wife departed, but Ekehu, once described by Charles Heaphy as 'the perfect bushman', was staunch. He and his wife stayed on, saving Brunner's life, and not for the first time. A little over two months later, Brunner was back in Nelson. He had completed an epic journey of exploration, the greatest by a Pakeha in New Zealand history.

Brunner was an unfathomable man. He was born into a middle-class life in Oxford, England, the son of a prominent attorney, one of seven children, but the only member of the family to emigrate. Yet he took the most extraordinary risks and endured unimaginable discomfort during his epic nineteen-month, 1846–48, journey from Nelson to just south of Franz Josef Glacier and back. He seems to have lacked a full understanding of the risks involved, even though he had been on a number of shorter expeditions over the previous five years. He was a surveyor who knew little about geology or botany and had none of the other professional obsessions that drove many explorers; although he recognised a seam of coal at the site of what became the Brunner Mine.

He would have survived for only a short time without his Maori companions. Evidence from his later life, during fairly inept work as an administrator, reinforces the impression that he was the antithesis of the careful planner and organiser that stamped the character of most successful explorers.

When Brunner left Nelson with his four Maori companions, he was carrying a load calculated at forty-five kilograms. Within three months he had run out of sugar, tea and flour, and from then on his diet consisted of some fish, eels, birds snared by his Maori companions, ground birds like weka, rats and fern-root. When they stayed at the mouth of the Grey River, they ate well on potatoes and fish courtesy of the local Maori, but during one period in the expedition when the party ran out of food they ate only rats for days on end; and during another they killed and ate Brunner's dog, Rover, which, he said, tasted like 'something between mutton and pork'.

'I believe I have now acquired the two greatest requisites of bushmen in New Zealand,' he wrote in his journal, 'viz. the capability of walking barefoot, and the proper method of cooking and eating fern-root . . . Now I can trudge along barefoot, or with a pair of native sandals . . . made of the leaves of flax . . .'

His journal is drenched with brief comments on the rain, of freshes spilling over riverbanks and forcing them up the hills, of the constant business of trying to keep dry or, mostly, to get dry after another wetting from the rain or a river. Early in the journey, he was sick for a few days but recovered. Then, two months from home, struck still by the paralysis, this indomitable man wrote in his journal: 'I had never before been any hindrance to the natives, always carrying my full share of the loads, and helping to get the firewood, etc . . . but Ekehu refused to leave me . . . I received great kindness from him and his wife for the week I was compelled to remain here, the woman attending me kindly, and Ekehu working hard to obtain food for us, always pressing upon me the best. He frequently told me he would never return to Nelson without me.'

That was 15 April 1848. A week later he wrote: 'Although I could only stand on one leg, yet I resolved to try and proceed. Ekehu had scoured the country, but could find nothing eatable within reach, and he would not leave for a night, so he carried my bed clothes forward some distance, and then came back, and partly by carrying and partly leading me, assisted me along.'

Even by 6 May, he would write: 'I again felt much pain in my side and was unable to use it; my eye and hand were even affected.' And on 15 May: 'I was also seized with a violent vomiting, which lasted all day and night, and my side gave me much pain. I attributed it to the badness of the living and exposure to the cold weather'. He doesn't mention his afflictions again in his journal but was still suffering from some paralysis when he arrived back in Nelson late in June.

Brunner was undoubtedly a brave and tough-minded man but he was lucky to have with him a guide as physically powerful and compassionate as Ekehu, and also his wife. They were members of the Rangitane iwi. Ekehu had been the guide early in 1846 when Brunner, William Fox, later a Premier, and Charles Heaphy, explorer, artist and soldier, mounted an expedition to search for grassy plains Maori had claimed existed over towards the West Coast. They were forced back by shortage of food.

Soon after their return, Brunner, Heaphy and Ekehu set out again on a journey around the coast, reached the mouth of the Grey River, the site of present-day Greymouth, and continued on to the Arahura River. Local Maori gave them information on the Greenstone trail over the Southern Alps but couldn't be persuaded to guide them. They returned via the coast, reaching Nelson in August. It was after this that Heaphy wrote his praise of the perfect bushman: 'Thoroughly acquainted with the bush, [Ekehu] appears to have an instinctive sense far beyond our comprehension . . . A good shot . . . A capital manager of a canoe, a sure snare of wild-fowl and a superb fellow at a ford, he is worth his weight in tobacco.'

On 11 December, less than four months after returning from the journey with Heaphy, Brunner and his Maori companions set out on foot on the nineteen-month expedition to traverse and examine new country through to South Westland and then perhaps to discover a pass through the Southern Alps to Canterbury. He carried with him a letter to William Deans of Riccarton in case he found a way to Port Cooper (Christchurch). In February 1848, before his illness set in, he climbed a peak somewhere between the Grey River and the Inangahua and glimpsed tussock land to the east, beyond Lewis Pass, and wanted to take that route, but his companions wanted to return to Nelson the way they had come.

On this great journey, he established the source and mouth of the Buller and Grey rivers, found the Hokitika River and walked on further south than any Pakeha had previously been, down past the Franz Josef Glacier. When he returned to what is now Greymouth, he spent nearly three months living with local Maori. His journal carries notes on Maori life and customs, but sketches he made were lost in a fire during his arduous return journey. His estimate of the Maori population on the West Coast was fewer than 100.

Brunner was twenty when he arrived in 1841 in Nelson Haven aboard the *Whitby* with the New Zealand Company's first party of settlers, led by Captain Arthur Wakefield. He served an apprenticeship as a survey assistant and undertook a number of walks exploring the Nelson–Motueka district from 1843. He moved to Canterbury for a few years after his epic journey but later became Chief Surveyor and Commissioner of Public Works to the Nelson provincial government. He was back on the West Coast during the 1850s to begin survey work for the towns of Westport and Greymouth.

He died a relatively young man in 1874, leaving his name indelibly on the landscape with Lake Brunner and the Brunner Range, both in the region he walked through. He also bequeathed to later generations an example of extraordinary courage and endurance.

Only recently has 'the perfect bushman', Ekehu, been recognised for his even more amazing stamina and his unstinting loyalty to a friend. The recognition began in the 1950s when Brunner's biographer, John Pascoe, wrote a verse for the *School Journal* that gave Ekehu some of the status he deserved as a partner in the enterprise. The poem begins with:

> *Brunner the bushman, the surveyor, the dog-eater,*
> *The young chap who fed himself off the land,*
> *Friend of Ekehu, hunter of birds,*
> *Eels, and the fern-root that grew in the rain.*

Not quite as amusing as the slightly inaccurate schoolboy jingle:

> *Thomas Brunner*
> *Did a runner*
> *Over the Southern Alps.*
> *He ran out of bread*
> *So ate rats instead*
> *For every little bit helps.*

Fourteen

THE GREAT QUAKE AND THE FUTURE OF WELLINGTON

Henry William Petre, second son of the eleventh Baron Petre, decided the country had no future for settlers after the 1855 earthquake had more or less razed the young town of Wellington and bounced and battered the Wellington and Wairarapa landscape, so he sold his house and farm at Woburn in the Hutt Valley and returned to England.

Petre, whose father was a director of the New Zealand Company, arrived in 1840 and had experienced an extraordinary number of severe quakes since then, this latest one on the night of 23 January, the day after settlers had celebrated the town's fifteenth anniversary. Geologists estimate the 1855 event as eight-plus on the Richter scale, vastly stronger than the more recent quakes in Murchison in 1929, Napier in 1931, Inangahua in 1968 and Edgecumbe in 1987, and certainly the biggest since Europeans arrived in the country.

After a lesser but nevertheless major earthquake in

1848, a number of settlers had left Wellington and the Hutt Valley; many of the 3000 inhabitants in 1855 also considered their future as aftershocks of varying degrees of intensity continued daily for more than a fortnight. Politicians Charles Bowen and Henry Sewell, who became Premier the following year, questioned whether the seat of government should ever be moved to Wellington, as was being considered. (Despite the apprehension, the town became the capital ten years later.)

Large areas of land in the region were raised. Two geologists, Tim Little and David Rodgers, said in 2005 they had found evidence that the mountains on the western side of southern Wairarapa moved eighteen and a half metres northwards, the longest horizontal movement ever recorded.

In his 2000 book, *Magnitude Eight Plus*, Rodney Grapes, Associate Professor of Earth Sciences at Victoria University, wrote: 'A few seconds before 9.17 pm, at a depth of twenty-five kilometres below Cook Strait, forty kilometres south-west of Wellington, a large section of the earth's crust suddenly ruptured, releasing an energy pulse 1000 times more powerful than the Hiroshima atomic bomb. The shock wave radiated outwards and upwards at a speed approaching six kilometres per second.'

In Wellington, brick chimneys toppled, walls collapsed, the façade of at least one building fell outwards, and the floor of every building was strewn with goods that had been stacked on shelves. Wooden houses were twisted and fissures opened in the streets, one of them oozing bluish grey mud. Estimates put the fatalities at lower than a dozen over the whole country but many in

Wellington suffered broken limbs and other injuries. The major reason for the low number of casualties was the small population – only 3200 people lived in Wellington at the time.

Pandemonium and panic reigned in the immediate aftermath, with most people living outside in tents refusing to go back indoors, despite clouds of dust billowing in the wind. More than one witness described the settlement as looking as though it had suffered a sustained cannon bombardment.

The quake was felt throughout the country. Damage was serious in Manawatu and the Wairarapa, and the north of the South Island. The beach around the south coast between Wellington and the Wairarapa was changed beyond recognition according to the few Europeans who had by then traversed it. It rose six metres.

Ten minutes or so after the first big jolt, tsunami swept across the isthmus between Cook Strait and Evans Bay, flooded Miramar Valley, raced through shops in Lambton Quay (which was closer to the shoreline then), pounded the beach at Palliser Bay and the Kaikoura coast, and sent waves surging up the rivers along the east coast of Marlborough and Canterbury. The water in Wellington Harbour rose an estimated two metres, flooding houses near the beach as well as the shops and sweeping across the ridge the quake had just thrown up that served as an improved road from the town to the Hutt Valley.

The European settlement of Wellington had been beset by nature's assaults from the beginning. The first pioneers to arrive in 1839 had decided to establish their town at Britannia, on the fertile, river-silt flats where Petone stands today. Exposure to the brisk winds that roar up the Hutt Valley from the south persuaded them to have the hills a few kilometres to the south-west surveyed. A severe flood that first winter removed any doubts and sent them scuttling around the harbour's edge to the present site of the city. But what worried Petre and others more was that earthquakes of some severity had occurred in the country, and especially around Wellington, every two or three years since the first settlers arrived, and nothing indicated they would desist. Petre believed that as people in Britain learned of this, immigration would stop.

Within a year of the arrival of New Zealand Company settlers, the first quakes occurred, followed by twenty-four more over the following five years. In 1843, a sharp jolt destroyed a number of buildings in Wanganui and killed a Maori couple beneath a landslip. A quake big enough to send Wellington residents racing from their houses in panic struck in 1846, and two years later came what could be called the little big one. A shock felt from as far north as East Cape and Taranaki and down through Banks Peninsula shook buildings and knocked walls over in Wellington, killing a soldier and his two children. Lieutenant-Governor Eyre said the quake and its long period of aftershocks threatened the existence of the settlement 'which will not easily recover'.

The exodus from Wellington in 1855 was, surprisingly, smaller than in 1848, perhaps because the death-toll estimate was only five or six. But had there been another big earthquake in the Wellington region within a decade of 1855, the effects on settlement would have been dire.

Henry Petre's son, Francis, born at Petone in 1847 immediately before the two big earthquakes that scared his father off, returned to New Zealand in 1872 and became the best-known New Zealand-born architect of his time. After supervising railway construction, he set up practice as an engineer and architect in Dunedin. He was a pioneer in the use of concrete, and among the many buildings he designed are the much-admired Cathedral of the Blessed Sacrament in Christchurch and the Catholic Basilica in Wellington.

Fifteen

GOLD, AND VIRTUE UNREWARDED

Central Otago was not the first place gold was found in New Zealand but it gave up what was called 'the colour' in such quantities and in such an accessible alluvial form that the news ignited the country's first prolonged gold rush. The discovery was notable, too, for the altruism of the man who made it, Tasmanian Gabriel Read.

Read was an experienced prospector who had worked the goldfields in California and Victoria but with only moderate success. He had gone home to Hobart from the Victorian fields, disenchanted with the unruliness of the miners. Violent clashes with the police exploded in the pitched battle at Eureka Stockade, near Ballarat, in which six policemen and more than twenty miners were killed. That was in 1854 but the animosity between the law and extremists continued for some years until Victorian yields dwindled in the late 1860s – in time for the Australians to ride the westerlies across the Tasman to join the rush to the new Westland fields that were the next stop for prospectors after Otago.

When Read heard of small finds in Otago, at Mataura and Lindis, he sailed for Dunedin and then walked up to Central to poke around the rivers there. In May 1861, in the eponymous Gabriel's Gully, he came to a place where foraging cattle had broken the banks of the Tuapeka River. With a spade, a tin dish and a butcher's knife, he collected seven ounces (nearly 200 grams) of gold in a few hours. He could have stayed and panned riches for himself, and must have considered that option, but instead reported the find to the Superintendent of Otago Province in Dunedin, and then returned with two companions, spearheading a rush of prospectors who fanned out across the countryside and ended what had been a prolonged economic slump in the province. The population of Otago jumped from 12,000 to 30,000 in the second half of 1861.

Gold had been discovered in the Coromandel and Collingwood, near Nelson, in the forties and fifties and in other parts of Central Otago, but not in the accessible quantities of Tuapeka and subsequent strikes nearby.

One of the first to visit the diggings at Tuapeka was a Dunedin storekeeper, John McIndoe, who wrote a report of ready riches for the *Otago Witness* less than a month after Read's initial report. He told of Read and his companions and a few other groups panning large quantities from the river. On his return to Dunedin, he said, he passed 'eight drays with all the necessaries for operation with a party of from four men to eight attached to each. In addition we met a number of foot passengers and riders hurrying on to the field so that by this time there will be a hundred diggers hard at work . . .

'Runholders, farmers and tradesmen are all preparing for or hurrying on to the diggings . . . I would also counsel the working men of Dunedin at once to make a start. They can easily make the journey on foot in two days. I have not the slightest fear of their being disappointed. Better to risk their chances than go idly about the streets of Dunedin.'

The gold panned from the rivers of Otago and a bit later in Westland enriched the whole country. In 1863, gold made up more than two-thirds of New Zealand exports, nearly three times as much as wool. The South Island boomed as prospectors flooded in at the rate of 1000 a day at the peak. Food producers and processors flourished, and heavy industry developed to support both cropping and mining, making Dunedin the most affluent and industrially advanced city in the country. Gold was a significant export earner for more than forty years, representing twelve per cent of earnings in the first decade of the twentieth century.

Read's altruism didn't stop at sharing his strike at cost to himself. When the rush was still at its height, he seemed more interested in teaching miners prospecting techniques and working as an arbitrator in settling disputes. He was later awarded £1000 by the provincial government, which fully understood the economic benefit of the gold, although some among the dour Presbyterian settlers had wanted the early discoveries kept quiet to avoid an incursion of faithless riff-raff.

Poor Gabriel returned to Tasmania, married his cousin, the widow of a clergyman, had no children and spent the last seven years of his life hospitalised with a mental illness. He received less from the provincial government than the men who discovered the Dunstan field and kept it a secret until they had panned a fortune for themselves. Thus is virtue rewarded.

The men who struck it rich at Dunstan, in the Upper Clutha, Horatio Hartley and Christopher Reilly, quietly worked away until they had amassed nearly forty kilograms of gold. When they took it back to Dunedin they revealed the source only after hard bargaining had cranked up a provincial government award. The *Otago Witness* reported in August 1862, when the Dunstan find was first announced: 'Building operations are almost at a standstill; clerks, craftsmen and labourers are all gone or going to the diggings.' Bakers shops were 'literally besieged' by those wanting portable food. Tentmakers, saddlers, clothiers and other merchants were wildly busy. 'As might have been expected, numbers of men have left their ordinary occupations, smitten with the general gold fever, and wages, as a natural consequence, are on the rise. The *Lombard*, bound for Auckland, not only was deserted by many of her passengers at Port Chalmers, but the crew also left the vessel.'

In November of that year, two shearers from a sheep station at Queenstown struck gold on the Shotover River's eastern bank at a place later named Arthurs Point after Thomas Arthur, one of the shearers. They took more than five kilograms from sand on the banks of the Shotover and Arrow rivers in just over a week, and in two months they earned £8000, a large sum at that time. News of the find triggered yet another rush during 1863.

With all these men living rough, nursing their gold lust, life was precarious enough, but the worst tragedy to hit them was in the early morning of 9 July that year, when a flash flood roared down the Arrow River, completely filling the gorge and washing away 100 miners to their death, carrying in the torrent their huts, tents, equipment and all their gold. It was one of the greatest disasters of early New Zealand history. Many shocked diggers left the goldfields for good.

Sixteen

THE CITY THAT NEVER WAS

On a summer's morning in 1862, hymns from 15,000 voices sprang into the air from London's East India Docks to farewell several hundred emigrants on their way to found a city in New Zealand.

Aboard the *Matilda Wattenbach* (969 tonnes) and the *Hanover* (1070 tonnes) were members of the country's third and last organised church settlement project. The Scottish Reformed Church had established Dunedin, and the Anglicans Christchurch, and now the Nonconformists were on their way to build the city of Port Albert, on the Kaipara Harbour north of Auckland.

The ships carried the first of the 1000 or more who had already subscribed to what the Reverend Landells of the London Tabernacle called 'one of the most remarkable emigration movements that have taken place in English history'. He compared the departing settlers with the Pilgrim Fathers on their way to New England two centuries before – a comparison not absurd, on reflection, when the religious persuasions of the two groups were considered.

The last hymn that summer morning was, ominously, 'Father through the Storm on Storm Appear'. It was sung at the end of a farewell that featured dozens of inspirational speeches, and was followed by 'Auld Lang Syne' and the firing of cannon as the ships were towed from the wharf. Most of New Zealand's early cities were built from organised settlement programmes but none of their pioneers got anything like as good a send-off as these ardent and enthusiastic Nonconformists. Eight ships carried about 3000 Albertlanders to New Zealand between 1862 and 1865.

And it all came to nothing.

The Albertland Special Settlement Association was the pet project of a British journalist, William Rawson Brame, not yet thirty and editor of the *Birmingham Mercury*. The son of a Baptist minister, he thought that the formation of a city in what was then Britain's favourite colony would be a fitting way in which to celebrate the bicentenary of the expulsion of the dissenting clergy from the Church of England and the consequent establishment of the Nonconformist movement.

For decades, waves of settlers had been moving from Europe, seen then to be overcrowded, to the United States and Canada. New Zealand had always attracted some but it was a much more arduous and expensive journey. The outbreak of civil war in the US made New Zealand and Australia more attractive destinations for settlers from 1861, so the Albertland project (named after Queen Victoria's consort) drew heavy press coverage. Soon, twenty-seven auxiliary committees were set up in many parts of Britain. Brame was appointed general manager and honorary secretary. He was an accomplished organiser and, while it would perhaps be unfair to label him corrupt, he never missed a chance to make money. The shipping company, Shaw Savill, paid him a five per cent commission on all passenger and freight charges, gave him and his wife free passage, and he negotiated a ten-shilling fee for each adult and five shillings for each child from the Auckland provincial government.

Both the *Matilda Wattenbach* and the *Hanover* had stormy 100-day journeys to Auckland, where they arrived just as the New Zealand civil war was warming up in the Waikato. The city was to be built on the shores in the upper reaches of Kaipara Harbour, with each Albertlander eligible to buy a town block and sixteen hectares of farmland. The town and district were gradually surveyed and subdivided but sales of land were disorganised and settlers who arrived were forced to live in tents until the mess was sorted out. When Brame arrived he was reviled, especially when he laid claim to some of the city subdivisions as recompense for money he claimed the Auckland provincial government had not paid him. He left unhappily for Auckland, where he died of a brain haemorrhage in March 1863.

The prospect of a major settlement was doomed. First, the notorious littoral drift on New Zealand's west coast meant that bars across the entrances to both the Kaipara and Manukau harbours, from which the supply ships were to set out, made shipping service notoriously unreliable. No land route from Auckland existed. In fact it was decades before an easy road north was built, and because of the situation of the west coast harbours, that side of the Auckland isthmus developed very slowly, except where the Auckland region expanded as far as Helensville.

Access for the Albertlanders was most commonly by sea up the east coast from the Waitemata to Mangawhai Harbour, followed by a rough overland journey across the roadless isthmus that was still heavily bushed and churned into mud in the winter. Forty-five years later, Wellsford, which eventually became the commercial centre for the region, was still not much more than a railway station and beleaguered by the wet winter weather. The *New Zealand Weekly News* reported in August 1908 that 'All around [the Wellsford station] and everywhere, east, west, north and south, is mud, treacherous slush that drags a pedestrian in up to the knees at every step.'

Much of the land bought for the Albertlanders was of poor quality and especially unsatisfactory for the sort of farming the inexperienced settlers undertook – growing wheat, for example. Some, according to the author of an excellent history of the settlement, JL Borrows, were so inexperienced and naïve they planted crops according to the English seasonal calendar. One new farmer planted split peas in his garden and couldn't understand why they didn't grow.

Some didn't bother to move north from Auckland once they landed and heard of the situation. Many others went to Port Albert but didn't stay, and some became community leaders in other settlements. The Albertlander who most distinguished himself was Henry Brett, later the proprietor of the *Auckland Star*. He was offered a job before he got off the *Hanover* and didn't continue on with the others. Another journalist who fell out with Brame was Samuel Johnson, who established the *Albertland Gazette* but left in 1864 as the settlement languished. Later, with his brother, he founded the *Marlborough Express*.

Some few did stay and eked out a living. Local Maori were helpful to the pioneers, generous with food and physical help, although some Waikato refugees from the war caused anxiety for a while. Kauri gum and flax became local industries for a few years, and the kauri trees themselves supported substantial milling companies until the resource ran out. Then a large amount of money was invested in tobacco growing. Next, tung oil trees were tried. They were native to China, and oil from the nuts had an industrial use in the manufacture of products such as paints and linoleum floor coverings. Both tobacco and tung failed. But gradually, over many years, the district attained affluence through fruit-growing and dairying.

Nowadays, Port Albert sits sleepily on the banks of the Oruawhare River, deep inside the tidal Kaipara Harbour, claiming a place in only the most detailed of atlases. As Maori knew very well, the Kaipara is a warm and pleasant part of the world, but no matter how hard-working or intelligent the settlers were, a port and a rich, accessible hinterland were essential to the growth and survival of a large settlement in the first half of the nineteenth century. The New Zealand Company, which also supported the Otago and Canterbury settlement associations, knew that to their very great advantage.

Seventeen

A MYSTIFYING AND SURREAL ENCOUNTER

The Battle of Gate Pa, the last set-piece battle in the Waikato–Bay of Plenty war between the British and Maori, remains a mystifying, surreal encounter, even after 140 years.

As the British ships disgorged troops and artillery pieces at Tauranga, Maori cast around for a place to build a pa to defend in what they realised was to be an inevitable battle. They reconstructed an old fort at a place called Waoku ('silent forest shade') on the edge of heavy bush. Their leader, Rawiri Puhirake, dispatched a formal message, notifying the British commander that they were ready and that, in order to lessen the fatigue of the British soldiers, they had prepared thirteen kilometres of road leading to the pa.

Along with the challenge to the British, Puhirake sent rules of fair play, setting up something like an Arthurian tournament. A Maori veteran, Hori Ngatai of the Ngaiterangi, in a memoir years later said: 'We drew up a challenge in the form of a letter to the British General inviting him to meet us and fight it out . . . All was excitement. The clansmen were busy preparing for the fray, making cartridges, sharpening tomahawks, cleaning guns, getting food supplies and so on. Martial councils were held and great war dances took place daily to put our young men in form and to arouse their warlike spirits.

'Our leaders drew up a code of regulations for the conduct of the fighting. It was resolved that barbarous customs should not be practised by us, that the wounded should be spared and the dead should not be mutilated. We resolved too that we should not harm non-combatants or unarmed persons. In short, to fight fairly and squarely on the same lines as the Pakeha. These regulations were put in by Rawiri Puhirake . . . For some time we waited for a reply to our challenges, but none came. We considered it very discourteous of the English that they did not even acknowledge that letter.'

Then as the weeks went by while the British reinforced the Tauranga garrison, the Maori leaders decided to construct a new position, settling on a site only a short walk from the British camp; so close they crept out at night to steal timber to cover their rifle pits from nearby stockyards and from a local resident's fence.

The pa was on Pukehinahina Ridge, atop a high bank above a ditch dug by the missionaries and on which they had placed a gate. Hence Gate Pa. The crest of the ridge had the harbour on one side and swamps on the other and at the rear, making it difficult for the British to use their superior numbers to surround it.

The Ngaiterangi achieved a remarkable feat of engineering in a short time. A veteran of the battle, Captain

Gilbert Mair, wrote: 'During the interval from the first occupation of Gate Pa, the rebels, energetically assisted by their women folk in the heaviest work, and being entirely unmolested, had converted a harmless-looking grassy knoll into a work that was to test the calibre of British troops to the utmost. Probably there never was an instance in modern warfare where more deliberate and carefully conceived plans had been devised for securing a crushing defeat of the enemy . . . The Gate Pa garrison never exceeded 230 men – General Robley is very emphatic on this point.'

One installation was large and another small, linked by a trench that was supposed to hold 600 Waikato warriors who never arrived. The main pa had an outer palisade and a complex of trenches, rifle pits and linking tunnels that enabled its occupants to survive a nine-hour barrage from eighteen artillery pieces. Mair wrote: 'During the several months our troops were stationed [at the Tauranga camp] prior to the actual hostilities, the Tommies, aye, all the officers too had closely fraternised with the hospitable and chivalrous Ngaiterangi, and a strong mutual regard and admiration had grown up between the two races; hence as the hour of battle drew nearer, none of the Imperial troops looked forward to it with eagerness and enthusiasm. Whether this feeling had any co-relation to the subsequent defeat I cannot say, but certain it is that the men had gloomy anticipations and all felt the deep seriousness and uncertainty of the adventure'.

The Ngaiterangi, the predominant tribe in the region, had committed no acts of rebellion against the Crown, but they were known to be supporters of the Maori King movement; so the government decided on a crushing, pre-emptive strike. All Maori to the west of Tauranga Harbour, Ngaiterangi territory, were declared to be dangerously sympathetic to the King movement. Those to the east of the harbour were declared friendly. It was true that the Ngaiterangi had sent their young men to fight alongside Waikato Maori in the wars there. These warriors had returned to their Bay of Plenty land and, despite defeats in the Waikato, knew only too well that their land was at issue. Meanwhile, an argument was going on among government officials. The commander of the British forces in Tauranga, Colonel Carey, had received instructions to destroy all the crops and livestock of Maori in the western region. However, the Civil Commissioner in Tauranga, Thomas Smith, wrote to the Colonial Secretary seeking a modification of the order, saying that such action would be extremely provocative and would ensure the total support of resistance by all Maori in the western region. He suggested, sensibly, that the military force's task should be to check on the movements of Waikato sympathisers but to take action only if it was forced on them against 'open rebels'.

Edward Shortland's reply was that of a pompous fool but Governor-General George Grey was much more sensible and circumspect.

On 21 January 1864, Maori looked on in what Captain Gilbert Mair described as 'friendly curiosity and wonderment' as three British men-of-war anchored off Tauranga Harbour; 700 troops were lightered ashore. Then the 68th Durham Light Infantry and the 43rd Regiment arrived on another vessel and set up an encampment with twelve- and six-pounder field pieces. More men arrived, including medical ambulance services. The

Maori realised that their alternatives were total surrender or a battle to defend their land.

On 21 April 1864, General Cameron and his staff arrived aboard HMS *Esk* and a few days later 600 marines and Naval Brigade troops disembarked. The guns, which now included a high-tech (for then) 110-pounder Armstrong and two forty-pounders, were emplaced about 400 metres from the pa. Not only did the British troops have heavy artillery support, but they were armed with the latest rifles against Maori muskets and double-barrelled shotguns, and they numbered nearly 2000 compared with the Maori force about an eighth of the size.

Late in the afternoon of 28 April, a sham attack was launched to cover for 600 men from the 68th Regiment under General Greer, who slipped along the beach at low tide and took up a position in the rear swamp to cut off any Maori retreat. At dawn the following day, the barrage opened up and the celebrated Battle of Gate Pa began. At first the guns were aimed ineffectually at a decoy flagstaff on a rise fifty metres to the rear of and well above the Maori positions. Later, though, the guns homed in on a corner of the pa and the palisade was breached.

Maori had in the pa a minister and a tohunga, both of whom blessed the warriors before the fighting started. Hori Ngatai said: 'One was a Christian named Ihaka, who fortified us with the rites of the Pakeha religion. The other was a heathen priest, one Te Wana, who performed the war rites of our forefathers and recited the olden time karakias for victory in the fight. So we were making things right with both sides – the Christian God and the Atuas of the Maori. It was all tino tika (very correct).

'The cannonade that morning began just as we were about to eat our meal of potatoes. Our Christian tohunga, Ihaka, clad in a white surplice, was standing up in a very conspicuous position invoking a blessing. Just as he uttered the words, "May the grace of our Lord Jesus Christ and love of . . ." a shell from one of the big guns struck him in the waist, and bursting, scattered his body all over the place . . . Panepane, one of our old men, a tattooed veteran, had leaned his gun against the earthworks while he joined in the prayers . . . He went to pick up his gun and found some of the dead minister's intestines were wrapped round and round the barrel, and a grim joke even at the cannon's mouth did the old warrior utter, "See, the white men even load and fire delicacies at us through their big guns".'

A few hours later, tohunga Te Wana was killed by cannon fire as he stood up high exhorting the defenders with traditional battle incantations.

At four o'clock, in heavy rain, a rocket was fired to signal the start of the assault with 300 troops from the 43rd Regiment and the Naval Brigade. The storming party went forward four abreast, two soldiers with two sailors flanked by their officers. They opened up with what Mair described as 'tremendous fire' and the 68th Regiment, at the rear of the pa, also moved forward, firing steadily. After only a few minutes the storming party at the front breached the defences and was inside the pa.

From within their underground shelters, which had preserved them from the artillery fire, the Maori were able to fire at the British from point-blank range. By then it was getting dark. Some Maori emerged and engaged the British in hand-to-hand fighting, leaving them disorientated. They ran in panic just as reinforcements sent by Cameron were approaching, compounding the confusion. Seasoned and courageous British troops had been spooked by the Maori resistance and fled in the most abject defeat to either side in the New Zealand Wars.

The British casualties in a short time were horrendous – thirty-eight were either killed outright or died soon afterwards of wounds; seventy-six were wounded, many severely. Maori casualties are not known with any precision but are believed to have been fewer than twenty-five.

What caused the British panic? According to Mair, a subaltern had called out, 'My God, here they come in the thousands,' as Maori who had tried to escape the pa through the rear were driven back into it by the 68th. Others told him the order 'Retire, Retire' was given. But it seems unlikely that the British troops would even have heard such calls in the confusion of the fight. Historians GW Rusden and James Belich portray the battle as won by a Maori trap the British fell into, that the British troops – complacent that the hours-long bombardment must have shattered the defenders – fled in disarray, traumatised by the sudden devastating fire from a largely unseen foe in their concealed positions. This seems a more likely explanation.

Their pa shattered and with the likelihood of assaults by even greater numbers the next day, the Maori, in small groups, crept through the lines of the 68th that night without loss. But before they left, they provided water for British wounded.

Eighteen

THE SECULAR SAINTS OF PARIHAKA

When Native Minister John Bryce and Colonel JM Roberts marched on Parihaka Pa in Taranaki at the head of 1600 troops in November 1881, they were doing what the great majority of Pakeha wanted them to do – lawfully suppressing a Maori rebellion. They would have had no idea they were marching into history as the symbolic villains of the decades-long battle between Maori and Pakeha over land.

As the years have passed, the mana of the Maori leaders at Parihaka, Te Whiti O Rongomai and Tohu Kakahi, has grown to something near secular sainthood, while Bryce has become damned as an obdurate, brutal and, some would say, stupid man.

Taranaki is where the land wars of the nineteenth century first blew up, in 1860, and where Titokawaru less than ten years later staged a revolt that for months ate at the self-confidence of colonial troops. Then, in 1878, Te Whiti and Tohu were blamed for inspiring passive resistance by Maori near Hawera who began ploughing settlers' land they claimed was theirs. At the time, Bryce described Parihaka as 'that headquarters of fanaticism and disaffection'.

By the late 1870s, the Waikato and Bay of Plenty had been largely subdued and the King Country encircled, but resistance had simmered away in Taranaki and, since 1879, Te Whiti had been conducting a passive campaign to claim land confiscated during the 1860s but not previously settled by Europeans. Te Whiti considered that all confiscated land in southern Taranaki that had not been developed should be returned to Maori. New Zealand's first Attorney-General, William Swainson, pointed out in 1859, on the eve of the Taranaki War, that settlers' land greed had gained them 53,000 hectares yet they had less than 18,000 hectares under cultivation. Twenty years on, Te Whiti and Tohu were trying to protect for themselves some of the formerly confiscated land about to go under the seemingly inexorable tide of Pakeha settlement.

Te Whiti ordered his people to pull up survey pegs, fence off what they considered was their land and seal off public roads, frustrating the work of government officials and the constabulary. Given Taranaki's recent history, alarm bells went off in New Plymouth only forty-two kilometres away and within the government in Wellington. As the passive campaign progressed, more than 100 Maori were arrested for obstructing the subdivision of the land for settlers and sent to the South Island where they were set to work building roads. The government had eased its own path towards oppression with legislation enabling the authorities to imprison protesters without trial.

The situation was one of great delicacy but no genuine attempt was made at mediation or diplomacy. To John Bryce, an incandescent Scot, the position was clear enough. The land had been confiscated 'legally', and the obstruction – passive though it may have been – was simply a rebellion that needed to be suppressed. Grounds for suspicion persist that those in the government who did not see the Maori behaviour as such a black-and-white issue were relieved that Bryce would do their dirty work for them.

He was born in Glasgow, came to New Zealand with his family at age seven in 1840, took up farming near Wanganui when he was twenty and remained on his property for fifty years until he retired to live in the town. During the Titokawaru insurrection in the late 1860s, he became a Lieutenant in the Kai-iwi Yeomanry Cavalry Volunteers, the position he said later he was proudest of in his long career. During this campaign, Bryce was involved in a charge against a group of Maori who proved to be unarmed children, two of whom were killed and others wounded. After some time in local government, he became a member of the General Assembly in 1866. He withdrew for reasons of ill health for a period and returned to represent Wanganui again in 1871. He was chair of the Native Affairs Committee from 1876 to 1879 and Minister for Native Affairs from 1878 to 1884.

The Pakeha population had grown spectacularly during the 1870s at the same time as Maori numbers were in decline. So the prevailing opinion was that Maori were no longer capable of mounting a serious threat to peace as they had twenty years before, but could still create a serious nuisance. Accordingly, during Bryce's term of office, the Native Department was wound down to save money, and the Native Land Court was given greater power to define Maori land by individual title and have it released for sale. All this suited Bryce's low tolerance for what he regarded as Maori recalcitrance, even though the British government had shown signs of unease at the government's Maori policy.

Te Whiti and Tohu knew that open insurrection would be disastrous for them and adopted the passive resistance policy, not, as sentimentalists would imply, simply because of spiritual goodness but mostly because it was the most effective policy available to them and because of their belief that one day, 'a day of reckoning', Pakeha would voluntarily just leave the country. Te Whiti had adopted this tenet from the teachings of Hauhauism. Every month, on the eighteenth day, Maori gathered at Parihaka in their hundreds to hear Te Whiti, their prophet, address them. Money was collected at Parihaka to fund Maori development after the Pakeha's departure.

By the late 1870s, Parihaka was the largest Maori community in the country. It had become a retreat for Maori from many parts of the country who had become dispossessed – refugees from Pakeha incursions on to their land. Te Whiti instructed the people not to fight back against the local constabulary as they fenced and ploughed land torn from them years before. At first, he was prepared to accept the opening up of the land on condition that adequate reserves for Maori were defined and publicised. The government proceeded without accepting this chance for peaceful compromise. Thus the Maori ploughing and disruption of surveyors were stepped up.

A new volunteer force was formed in Taranaki and commenced training. The government then established a commission to investigate the Taranaki land issue. Te Whiti refused to cooperate but continued to advocate only passive opposition. The next move by the government was to use troops under Colonel Roberts to build roads. They moved cautiously forward in military style as though an attack was a possibility.

No bids were made when the government offered land at Parihaka for sale in February 1881 and the Taranaki newspapers, reflecting popular sentiment, were demanding firm action to make the area safe for settlers. With a general election not far off, the government decided on a show of power. By late October, thirty-three units around the country were called up for active service. An intimidating force to quell Maori aspirations – 1000 armed volunteers and 600 members of the Armed Constabulary – converged on Rahotu, five kilometres from Parihaka. Issued with two days' rations and forty rounds of ammunition per man, this huge force, led by Bryce and Roberts, marched on the village on 5 November and was confronted not by an army but by singing children. Nevertheless, the Riot Act was read.

Te Whiti was a man of great character and commanding appearance who had taught his people to be sober, to work hard and to face their situation with courage and restraint. He led by example. According to the historian Hazel Riseborough, he 'acted calmly and with restraint in the face of what government ministers often described privately as deliberate goading . . . All he wanted was to remain at peace on his ancestral land.'

Te Whiti and Tohu were arrested and sent to New

Plymouth, escorted by a squad of the Taranaki Mounted Rifles. Then, in an act of vandalism, Bryce ordered the village to be demolished. Later, crops were destroyed and livestock killed in a bid to disperse the villagers.

Te Whiti and Tohu were allowed to return to Parihaka after sixteen months. The authorities assumed their mana was broken but Te Whiti soon rebuilt his leadership and, when the government resumed its investigation into the land question, the civil disobedience campaign was resumed. As a result, he and Titokowaru, who was living at Parihaka, were jailed for several months in 1886. Some Maori were kept without trial for years and some never returned.

Over the twenty years after Te Whiti finally returned, he and his supporters rebuilt the village as a stylish and modern small town, and it exists today; but the chances of a large Maori community flourishing there were thwarted by the lack of surrounding land. Land claims for the area remain unresolved.

Bryce, backed by the government and the majority opinion of colonists, won the battle but history has given the verdict clearly to the people of Parihaka. Bryce is remembered as a man severely limited by his lack of imagination and inability to compromise. Throughout his career, he would resign from posts on principle, fulminating at opposition.

Tohu and particularly Te Whiti are enshrined in our culture as men of courage, undaunted by the violence used against them, offering an example of how they were prepared to live in peace given the land they needed to support themselves. They are symbolic victims of a time when many of the settlers believed in the divine superiority of the British race and culture. Their remarkable gesture of peaceful defiance has been expressed by poets and playwrights, by painters and musicians, and become one of the most elevating tales from New Zealand history.

Footnote: In 1883, a three-volume *History of New Zealand* by GW Rusden was published in London and contained a passage about the attack on Maori women and children during the campaign against Titokawaru by the Kai-iwi Yeomanry Cavalry Volunteers, led by Lieutenant John Bryce. This and other accounts in the book of injustices against Maori incensed the government of the time. On the word of the Bishop of Wellington, Dr Hadfield, Rusden included women among those attacked. It was later established that no women had been present, so Bryce sued Rusden for libel. No one contested that unarmed children were killed, but the government was furious that Rusden had made them seem barbaric in their treatment of Maori, and at one stage considered paying Bryce's legal fees.

The case was heard in London where the New Zealand Premier at the time of the incident, Sir John Hall, gave evidence in favour of Bryce. Rusden claimed he had been misinformed by a reputable source (Dr Hadfield) and had not intended to mislead. The judge directed the jury that the fact that no women were present was fundamental. Nothing else mattered. The jury awarded Bryce £5000. *The Times* wrote: 'The penalty for writing contemporary history has rarely been so heavily paid.'

Rusden's history was republished in 1895 without the offending material. I have copies of both editions.

When I went to read the 1883 edition that was subject to the libel, I discovered the pages were uncut. A hundred years after it was published, no one had read it.

Nineteen

GOD SAVE THE HAWERA REPUBLIC

Eighteen years after the secession of eleven southern states from the United States of America, the Republic of Hawera seceded from the Colony of New Zealand and elected its own President, James Livingston.

Or did it?

As we have seen in Chapter 18, in 1879 Te Whiti O Rongomai and Tohu Kakahi were passively resisting the surveying and subdividing of land for European settlement on the Waimate Plains in South Taranaki. Surveyors with armed escorts moved on to the plains in 1878 to divide them for farmer-settlers and to stake out a coastal road. Because all went well, the armed escort was dispensed with. In March the following year Maori from Te Whiti's base at Parihaka interrupted the survey and moved the instruments and equipment back across the Waingongoro River. They refused to allow the surveyors to return. At that same time, on two sites near New Plymouth, Maori moved on to

112

settlers' land and began to plough it up.

Everyone, including the Premier Sir George Grey, said the situation was highly flammable, even though Te Whiti, Tohu and Titokowaru, then living at Parihaka, had said they would not fight. The trouble was self-proclaimed pacifist Titokowaru had, less than a decade before, fought a series of battles over land issues against numerically greater colonial forces and won spectacular victories.

On 6 June 1879, 300 jittery settlers held a public meeting in Hawera and warned the government of the unprotected condition of the Hawera and Normanby settlements; the absence of any organisation of the settlers to draw together in case of disturbances; their alarm at the ploughing of settlers' land near New Plymouth; and the lack of an immediate government response to prevent a collision between the two races.

Next, the Commander of the Patea Armed Constabulary, Major Noake, arrived to organise a volunteer corps in the Hawera District, and the following day 180 infantry and ninety cavalry volunteers paraded. Trouble was, they didn't have enough guns to go around and some of the arms they did have were described as suitable only for the Sydney Museum. Noake appointed Captain PG Wilson as Commander of the Hawera Cavalry and Captain James Livingston as Commander of the Hawera Rifle Corps.

A large number of Maori were gathering at Te Whiti's base at Parihaka, so the rumour went, so settlers furthest from Hawera moved to town for safety. Then the Maori crossed the Waingongoro River and began to plough up Livingston's front lawn. Still the Maori showed no signs of aggression. Local historian Pam Bromley described what happened as: 'A settler had a quiet chat to the Maoris and said that the Europeans did not wish to interfere in the dispute respecting the Plains but that "they would not suffer the proceedings as were going on".'

The Maori ploughmen came back on 22 June, were again escorted back across the bridge over the river, and were said by Bromley to 'have accepted the situation with considerable grace'.

However, on 23 June the Maori ploughmen returned. They were met by nervous and exasperated settlers who removed them peaceably to the bridge where they were 'met by Captain Wilson and his troop of Light Horse in skirmishing order'. The Maori went quietly. Elated by their success in the face of a dilatory government response, settlers held another public meeting that night and Livingston was elected captain of what was called an 'ejectment committee'. But then the crisis petered out, although Wilson's Hawera Light Horse and parties of armed constables patrolled the area and arrested a few groups of ploughmen.

When the government troops finally arrived on 10 July, Livingston, presiding at yet another public meeting, read out a telegram from Grey congratulating all concerned. The meeting, however, so adamantly disagreed with Grey's previous assessment of the district's defence needs that they sent a deputation to Wellington to make their point.

While the crisis was alive, the *Wanganui Herald* started referring to the Republic of Hawera as a joke, but the joke began to be taken seriously and thirty-five years later the 'Republic' had become part of the town's mythology. On

James Livingston's seventy-fourth birthday, in 1914, the *Hawera Star* began a report of a birthday gathering with: 'It was a unique gathering that assembled at Hawera on Monday to do honour to Mr James Livingston, who, in 1879, was declared the duly elected President of the Hawera Republic, which had then declared its independence.

'The reason for this proceeding was that the Maoris were becoming very troublesome, under the tutelage of Te Whiti and Tohu, the two reigning chiefs at Parihaka, which was then attracting Natives from all parts of the North Island and many districts of the South Island as well, even the Chatham Islands, contributing their quota at times to the large monthly gatherings at the foot of Mt Egmont. The Natives, not content with holding the Waimate Plains and other lands north of the Waingongoro River, which had been confiscated owing to the owners' participation in the war, wherein Titokowaru distinguished himself, crossed the river and began ploughing up settlers' land.

'Repeat petitions were made to the Grey government for protection from Native oppression and, as none was forthcoming, a meeting was held and the settlers, in solemn conclave, passed a resolution declaring Hawera a Republic, and James Livingston was elected President. The settlers then took measures for their own defence and placed guards in front of the President's house, as his land was the first to be ploughed up.'

After a change of government and the appointment of a new, tough Defence Minister in October, the *Hawera Star* continued, 'The infant Republic gradually faded out of existence, and its President was only too glad, like

George Washington, to devote himself to agricultural and pastoral pursuits.'

Satire? Not a bit of it. Deadly serious stuff, it was.

Livingston's seventy-fourth birthday was also reported in the *Evening Post*, and it does seem as though he was something of a hero. The *Post* referred to 'the Republicans of Hawera', and said Livingston had been present at Te Ngutu-o-te-Manu when Titokowaru achieved his most spectacular victory over the colonists, the battle in which the fabled Forest Ranger Gustavus Von Tempsky was killed. A Colonel Roberts claimed that if it had not been for Livingston's 'bush craft, pluck and coolness, it was very doubtful whether any of them would have got away'.

From that birthday in 1914 for fifty years or so, the Republic of Hawera moved from fantasy to fact. In the *Encyclopaedia of New Zealand*, published by the government in 1966, historian Bernard Foster gave the republic a modicum of credence when he called the whole incident 'a mildly amusing political extravaganza. It existed to meet an emergency and lasted only until government aid reached the district. The Republic was a popular movement − a "res publicae" in the classical sense. From the point of view of international law it could never have received recognition as an independent state because it possessed only a western frontier − the Waingongoro River.'

Twenty

A COLD COLLATION FOR JESUS COLLEGE

One day in 1882, in Jesus College, Cambridge, JCN Grigg entertained the college rowing eight at lunch. He had thawed, cooked and then served two cold hindquarters of lamb from Longbeach, the celebrated Canterbury farm owned by his father, John Grigg. His guests loved it and most had three helpings, reported Grigg, the son. He told them they had enjoyed meat from his father's farm, shipped as part of the first refrigerated cargo from New Zealand. A biographer of Grigg the father, PG Stevens, who tells this story, claims the son was 'the first man to eat Canterbury lamb in England'. The *Dunedin* had left Port Chalmers in February that year and successfully carried the cargo to London through the spoiling heat of the tropics. What the Cambridge men also would not have known but what the Griggs, father and son, may have suspected was that the technological development of refrigerated shipping would have a greater influence on the economic future of New Zealand than any other single discovery.

Although John Grigg was chairman of the recently incorporated Canterbury Frozen Meat Company, the only Longbeach meat aboard the *Dunedin* was three Shropshire-cross lambs and two wethers. The bulk of the cargo had come from New Zealand and Australia Land Company farms, whose London-based manager, William Saltau Davidson, had masterminded the *Dunedin* trial shipment. The man who made it physically happen was the company's superintendent in New Zealand, Thomas Brydone, who had supervised the killing and dressing of the meat. A killing shed had been erected at the company's Totara Farm, near Oamaru, and six butchers worked from four o'clock each morning to get the kill on the morning train for Port Chalmers, where the carcases were taken aboard the *Dunedin* and frozen between decks on the ship before being stowed in the hold.

A hero of the journey to England was the ship's master, Captain Whitson, who had to contend with a fire in the sails ignited by the machinery and, when the cold air failed to circulate adequately as the vessel sailed through the tropics, had to crawl into the hold to cut new air ducts. He was overcome by the cold and would have died there had not the first officer crawled in behind him, fastened a rope to his leg and pulled him free.

The *Dunedin*, a 1200-ton sailing ship operated by the Albion Shipping Company, left Port Chalmers on 11 February, two months after the first carcase was ceremoniously stowed by Davidson, and arrived in London on 24 May, where she was met and her cargo inspected – by Davidson. The trial had cost £1000, and proved worth every penny. The 4908 prime sheep and lamb carcases sold within a fortnight for £8000, more than twice the price they would have fetched in New Zealand.

The Times of London, in a special editorial, said the enterprise was 'a feat which must have a place in commercial – indeed in political – annals.'

In the twenty years from 1871, when old sheep were being killed and buried as waste once the last fleece had been taken from them, until 1891, almost a decade after the frozen meat trade started, sheep numbers increased from just under ten million to seventeen million and were still growing fast.

The coming of refrigeration could hardly have been better timed for New Zealand. The early 1880s were bleak as the country lay in the cold clutches of an economic slump. Wool prices had been falling since the 1870s. Wool was the only value sheep provided, and wool and wheat were the only substantial agricultural exports. Tens of thousands of immigrants had flocked to the colony in the 1870s as Colonial Treasurer Julius Vogel's programme of huge borrowing for infrastructure lured them from Britain and Australia. A decade later, colonists were leaving for Victoria or the United States and more would have gone had they been able to afford it. Some attempted to get government help to emigrate.

Although farming techniques were improving rapidly in Britain and railways had eased distribution from the country to the towns, the population was increasing as never before – by twenty-five per cent to thirty-five million between 1850 and 1880. New Zealand's population had grown spectacularly too, from 115,000 to half a million in the same period, but not as fast as sheep and cattle numbers. So the Americas, Australia and New

Zealand were so abundantly oversupplied with meat that in some places it was worthless; whereas shortages in Britain and other high-population European countries kept prices there high, and the poor went hungry. The trick was to get meat from the superabundant sources to the high-demand markets. Prices would come down but the market would grow accordingly.

The truth is that New Zealand lagged behind in the technological drive to export meat. Australians had been sending canned meat to Britain since the 1850s and their entrepreneurs had developed a technique of exporting boned meat packed in lard. New Zealanders worked on similar programmes and quality canned meat was exported. By 1880 Britain had imported sixteen million pounds weight of canned meat from Argentina, the United States, Australia, and including a small amount from New Zealand.

If the surfeit of mutton was the main problem, beef was in oversupply too. Alexander Bathgate of Dunedin wrote in his *Colonial Experiences* as early as 1874: '. . . the Cockatoos used to do very well from the sale of their cattle, but as the country has become more fully stocked up, cattle have greatly depreciated in value, and were a year or two ago literally unsaleable'. And that was despite the population increase Otago had experienced during and after the gold rush.

From early in the nineteenth century, scientists around the world worked on finding an efficient and reliable mechanical method of freezing perishable produce and keeping it frozen on the long journey to Europe from distant sources of supply. Efficient technology was essential because ships had to sail through the heat of the tropics. The French were first. In 1877, two ships were fitted with refrigeration machinery and carried frozen meat from Argentina to France. However, then as now, French farmers were well protected from foreign competition, so the trade did not thrive. The next move was from Australia, where a cool store had been set up in Sydney's Darling Harbour as early as 1861. A bid to send frozen meat in 1876 failed. But in 1880, the *Strathleven* reached England with a cargo in good condition from Queensland, and an industry was born.

William Saltau Davidson was a Scot, the son of a banker, who had come to New Zealand as a cadet with the Canterbury and Otago Association, in which his father had bought shares. At the age of twenty he arrived at Port Chalmers and began work as a shepherd on The Levels, a station at Timaru owned by the association. He quickly rose through positions of greater and greater responsibility until, after twelve years in the colony, he returned to Scotland as manager of the New Zealand and Australia Land Company. He vigorously investigated techniques for preserving meat, including refrigeration, and all the time he encouraged experiments designed to develop sheep breeds adapted especially for the New Zealand environment. He also sent Danish experts to the company's dairy factory at Edendale, in Southland, to put cheese-making on an industrial basis.

Davidson and Brydone got it right first time with refrigeration. Davidson organised the shipping service, the financial support, and later became deeply involved in the ancillary businesses of finance and insurance that quickly sprang up around the frozen meat industry. He wasn't alone. Big-thinking, innovative farmers with large estates, like John Grigg, put a lot of energy into frozen-meat exports which, within a decade, brought a wave of prosperity to New Zealand on which the Liberal government rode into office and stayed there for more than fifteen years. Ten years after the *Dunedin* trial, other ships had been fitted out with the refrigeration machinery (most of them steamships), and seventeen freezing works had been established capable of handling three and a half million carcases a year. By 1911, thirty-one works were scattered around the country.

It took dairying longer to exploit the new technology fully. A small experimental consignment of butter from Edendale was also aboard the *Dunedin* and arrived in excellent condition. A larger amount went a year later and, by 1890, butter and cheese made up more than seven per cent of export earnings. Milk production and processing – based on small family farms, most of them seriously undercapitalised and many isolated by bad roads – took longer to develop than meat production and processing, but became a mainstay of the economy as the industry matured.

The die was thus cast for New Zealand farming. Until Britain entered the European Common Market ninety years after the *Dunedin's* epic voyage, farmers produced a narrow range of products – mainly meat and dairy products – and bulk-shipped them to the British market. The national economy rose and fell depending on prices on the other side of the world but, by and large, the arrangement brought a high level of prosperity to New Zealand.

Twenty-one

THE RUSSIANS WERE COMING

Not long after dawn in the late spring of 1885, the 'cruiser' *Hinemoff* sailed into the Hauraki Gulf. Four kilometres from the artillery battery at Fort Cautley, she came under heavy fire. Thousands of Aucklanders lined Mt Victoria, and units of volunteers from as far as Waikato gathered on Queen Street Wharf, at Fort Resolution, in the Domain, and at other assembly points, preparing to repel Russian sailors and marines. The *Hinemoff* got past Cautley, veered towards Fort Resolution to pour a broadside at the defenders, and then straightened up to sail into Waitemata Harbour. But as she passed through the Rangitoto Channel, an electro-observation mine was triggered and blew her to pieces.

Well, that's how the newspapers described the biggest and most hilarious of the exercises at many of New Zealand's major ports during the 'Russian Scare' of the 1880s. The *Hinemoff* was the government-owned steamer *Hinemoa* under the command of Captain Fairchildoffsky, alias Fairchild. The event took place on the Prince of Wales's birthday, 9 November.

Exercises were held in other centres, as late as 1887 in Otago. They were all watched by crowds of local citizens spread around the high ground like golf galleries; although, in places where army and navy officers and some of the civil authorities wore all their ribboned, braided finery, the occasion more closely resembled an opera.

Since the Crimean War between Britain and Russia in the early 1850s, the foreign policy interests of the two powers had overlapped in places like Afghanistan. Tension continued as the two countries several times came to the brink of war. The scare waves reaching New Zealand were strong enough by 1859 for the government to accept an offer from Ngati Whatua of land on the harbour edge for the defence of Auckland against the impending invasion.

Once the Russians had been demonised as enemies of the British, the hypothesis was that, in the event of war, Russian ships would descend on the largely undefended ports of Australia and New Zealand. Scenarios included capturing and looting merchant vessels, invading cities and looting the bullion in banks, or holding the citizenry to ransom.

The anxiety was enthusiastically promoted by the Governor-General, Sir William Francis Drummond Jervois, a glowering former member of the Royal Engineers and an expert on colonial defence systems; and by other military men, including General Sir George Whitmore, a veteran of the Land Wars, particularly in the campaign against Te Kooti; and Britain's Colonial

Secretary in the Grey Ministry of 1877–79. Jervois, having compared New Zealand defences adversely with those of the Australian colonies, declared in a number of reports and speeches that:

- New Zealand should anticipate a raid by a force of three vessels at most, one at least being ironclad.
- Main ports should be capable of defending themselves, leaving British naval ships to fight raiders at sea.
- Fortifications should consist of heavy ordnance, torpedo boats, mines, and well-trained volunteer troops.
- The cost for guns and undersea mines to protect the ports of Auckland, Nicholson, Lyttelton, Chalmers and Bluff would be, he estimated, £400,000, plus 'some annual expenditure for maintenance, ammunition and stores, and for the pay of officers and men', which he said was: 'A moderate price for the benefit it will purchase . . . It is not only impolitic, but rash for her [New Zealand] to remain in a passive, defenceless state, unprepared to resist aggression, trusting to the forbearance of any Power possessing the means of attack.'

Whitmore, a slim, small-boned man with a beard that curved from his chin like a straw brush, had fought the Russians at Sevastopol as a young man. As the anti-Russian jitters grew, he was appointed Commandant of the Colonial Defence Force and Commissioner of the Armed Constabulary. He was convinced the 'Russkis' were the main New Zealand enemy, and neither he nor any of the others involved made any effort to hide their jingoistic anti-Russian feelings in the interests of diplomacy.

Perhaps to distract New Zealanders from the severe economic depression they were enduring at the time, politicians and old soldiers, aided by the newspapers, had unabashedly talked up the Russian Scare for more than a decade, especially since the Russians had bought warships from the United States.

The mood was captured vividly by Ewen William Alison, a successful Auckland businessman, Mayor of Devonport in the 1890s, and later in life an inveterate chronicler of his time. His family had a connection with the sea as operators of the Waitemata Harbour ferry services. In *A New Zealander Looks Back*, he wrote of the 1880s: 'I have a vivid recollection of a Devonport youth dressed in the uniform of a Naval Volunteer. He carried a rifle over his shoulder and a bayonet at his side. New Zealand was in the jitters.

'There was impassioned talk of a Russian invasion, and my youthful friend in his naval uniform was proceeding to the parade ground; and he looked proud of himself as one of the young colony's defenders. New Zealand was then forty-five years of age, and there was talk of war, serious talk of war. As a youngster I was frightened. I did not want any foreign army to land and take our little country.'

Wellington's *Evening Post* editorialised in March 1885: 'It may, we think, be taken for granted that if war does ensue, Russia will attempt to strike a blow at English and colonial commerce in South Pacific waters . . . Whatever vessels she sends to these waters, will be regularly commissioned ships of war . . . swift, lightly armed vessels . . .' The search for coal would lure them to a New Zealand port, the newspaper continued, 'but the temptation to demand a ransom would probably be too great . . . It would not be in human nature to refuse to avail themselves of the opportunity to demand a "subsidy" to refrain from burning or pillaging.' And so a small nervous nation, egged on by Russophobes, held its harbour exercises.

Not everyone lost their sense of humour, though. According to Glynn Barratt, author of *Russophobia*, the *Patea Mail* canvassed for rifle recruits 'in prospect of a war between Russia and Patea'.

An easing of tension between Britain and Russia had occurred in 1881. Taking advantage of the moment of calm, *Afrika*, a cruiser from the Russian Far East Squadron, visited Auckland in the course of a voyage around the Pacific Rim. Vice Admiral Aslanbegov reported: 'The reception given to us in New Zealand was polite in the highest degree. But the desire to inspect a Russian cruiser was wonderful . . . boats overflowing with the public drew alongside us, and there were days when the number of visitors exceeded a thousand . . .'

All very civilised. What he didn't seem to notice was an article in the *New Zealand Herald*: 'Had the Russian cruiser *Afrika*, which reposes peacefully on the waters of the Waitemata, come in hostile guise, what then? Had she run out her guns and sent a boat ashore demanding a ransom with the threat of a bombardment if it were refused, what then?. . . We shall have to pay or suffer – suffer in pocket and suffer ignominy – from such weak craft as the Russian cruiser . . . This colony has done nothing but *talk*, and it is possible that nothing but disaster will induce its rulers to protect its shores.'

Within a month of the *Afrika*'s departure, relations between London and St Petersburg deteriorated again and fear and consequent chauvinism reasserted itself.

Since its birth as a nation at Waitangi, New Zealand anxiety had been aroused by French intrusion into the Pacific, then by German commercial interests in Samoa, along with the Yellow Peril and the Russkis. On the day of the *Hinemoff* attack, proceedings were closely watched by a German officer, Kapitan Karl Schmidt, a guest of General Whitmore. According to Barratt, Schmidt 'learned with interest that one detachment of Navals had successfully stormed Albert Park in Auckland's centre, even hoisting the "detested Russian flag"'.

Oh dear, enemies were everywhere.

Footnote: Jervois and Whitmore had their way. Auckland was heavily fortified as the Russian Scare lingered on. Cannon were installed at Forts Bastion, Resolution, Cautley, Takapuna and Victoria. The most powerful was a fourteen-ton, eight-inch breach-loading 'disappearing' gun, which is still in place on Mt Victoria. When the fort was closed in 1925, the gun was greased and partially buried in scoria; it was restored in the late twentieth century for reasons of historical interest. Its barrel was almost twenty feet long and a charge of 110 pounds of black powder could fire a shell up to five miles. Practice targets were installed on Rangitoto.

However, the gun was only ever fired once and caused

great damage. No one seems to remember what happened to the shell – but the percussion broke a lot of windows in Devonport.

Twenty-two

THE CANOE MESSAGE FROM ATUA

Guide Sophia, who conducted tours of the fabled Pink and White Terraces, was one-name famous in June 1886 when Mt Tarawera blew up, and she sheltered many of those who survived the debris that crushed so many houses in the area. Sophia – a short black pipe clamped in her mouth below tumbling black hair, a wide brow, thin nose and small moko on her lips – was a commanding figure. Born at Kororareka, the daughter of Kotiro Hinerangi and Alexander Gray, a blacksmith from Aberdeen, she was educated at a Methodist Church school in Auckland. She was a witty and fluent raconteur, at ease in both English and Maori.

For fifteen years, Guide Sophia regularly set out from the tourism village of Te Wairoa, with its two hotels, to visit the terraces, accompanying groups of tourists, many of whom were foreign celebrities who had made long sea journeys to come to one of the world's most distinctive attractions. The delicately coloured, fretworked beauty of the terraces had been wrought over hundreds of years by silicon and steam. But they were destroyed in one explosive night by the geothermal activity that had created them.

The White Terraces, looking as though carved from marble, descended thirty metres to the shore of Lake Rotomahana – a series of stepped basins filled with water, boiling where it emerged from springs at the top and warm at the bottom. Silicon and carbonate sediment lined the rock as the water spilled down each level. Visitors could climb some way up, wading through basins varying in depth. The terraces spread like an open fan covering three hectares. They were described by one early visitor as 'a crystal staircase, glittering and stainless . . .'

The Pink Terraces – created by the same process but on the far side of the lake – were tinted a salmon pink with patches of pale yellow. Tourists could undress among shrubs alongside and then bathe in one of the smooth-surfaced basins, shallower than the White Terraces opposite and jutting further out over the basins below. The pink fan covered two and a quarter hectares.

The tall, rocky ridges of Tarawera rise from a geothermal region that has erupted from many vents over the past few thousand years, and yet no one in the nineteenth century recognised it as a volcano, perhaps because it had no symmetrical cone and no obvious crater. When it blew through gaping fissures along the crumpled landscape on 10 June 1886, very little lava spilled but massive volumes of mud and rocks were flung into the air or rumbled down the sides, erasing the famous terraces and killing 153 people in the three mainly Maori settlements of Te Wairoa, Te Ariki and Moura. Sophia and about fifty people survived in Te Wairoa by taking shelter in her small, sturdy house with its high-pitched roof. She forbade them from fleeing. A few others in Te Wairoa found refuge in other buildings that remained partially upright in a sea of ash and mud, but all the people in Te Ariki and Moura, and some Maori caught on islands in Lake Rotomahana, were buried in deep graves under thousands of tonnes of volcanic debris.

The eruption was accompanied by a pyrotechnic display of such brilliance a number of those who saw it painted it in retrospect as skyscapes flashing with fire.

Some people in the central North Island stayed up late on 9 June to watch an occultation of Mars. From 10.20 p.m. the planet began to disappear behind the moon. Two hours later a series of violent earthquakes began to spin out concentrically from around the base of the massif surrounding Tarawera. At their worst, the quakes were felt more than 160 kilometres away, and locals couldn't hold their feet. During the eruptions, people as far away as Auckland thought the noise was distant cannon fire.

At 1.30 a.m. a dome called Wahanga ejected a mixture of basalt scoria and rhyolite, followed by an eruption from Ruawahia, a central dome, and then the main Tarawera vent exploded, sending up a mushroom cloud carrying stones and mud high into the air above scoria so hot it welded together and formed small lava flows. Then the whole area of Lake Rotomahana and fissures running for fourteen kilometres blew up. The mud and ash from this eruption became the topsoil for the surrounding 12,000 hectares, and ash dusted land more lightly over 16,000 square kilometres. After the initial eruption and until about mid-morning, the darkness was intense. Dawn was obliterated.

In terms of geological time, this was a continuation of activity that had ripped the region apart. About 26,000 years ago, one of the world's biggest-ever eruptions left Lake Taupo as its crater. Four thousand years ago, Taupo blew again, this time on a smaller scale, and some time around the turn of the thirteenth to the fourteenth century Tarawera blew in what was the largest eruption since human settlement in New Zealand. Later, the government geologist estimated that in this eruption Tarawera ejected slightly less than a third of the volume of volcanic ash that Krakatoa had sent spinning into the atmosphere only three years before.

The 1886 cataclysm created its own legends. For some time before the eruption, Sophia and others had been disconcerted by the rising and falling lake levels, by the erratic behaviour of geysers, and by an apparition that appeared on Lake Rotomahana. Ten days before the eruption, Sophia set out across the lake to take a party of tourists to visit the terraces. Six Maori paddlers and three Maori women were aboard along with a physician, Dr Ralph, from Melbourne; Father Kelliher, a Catholic priest from Auckland; Mr and Mrs Sise and their daughter from Dunedin; and a Mr Willie Quick from Auckland. They had travelled about two kilometres when they saw a war canoe with some of the Maori occupants paddling and others standing. Their bowed heads were crowned, so the Maori in Sophia's party claimed, with feathers that were emblems of death. Less than a kilometre from the tourists' boat, the war canoe faded and then disappeared.

The Europeans all claimed they saw it. Mrs Sise described it and Father Kelliher drew it. The occupants of another tourist boat on the lake also said they saw it and one of them, Mr Josiah Martin from Rotorua, later drew it from memory.

The local Maori claimed that no such war canoe existed in the district. It was, they said, a message of impending death from the spirit world – from atua.

Slight local earthquakes had been going on for decades but they had grown in frequency and intensity since the 1840s. Geologist Ferdinand Hochstetter had noted twenty-seven years earlier that Maori had once lived densely on the shores of Lake Rotomahana but most had gradually left because of the increasing frequency of the earthquakes and because of the erratic rising and falling of springs.

As for Sophia, she later became the pre-eminent guide at Whakarewarewa, Rotorua, and the year before she died, in 1911, was painted by Charles F Goldie.

Twenty-three

THE SERMON THAT MOVED A NATION

The Reverend Dr Rutherford Waddell was angered by poverty and exploitation, so one Sunday in October 1888 he preached a sermon on 'the sin of cheapness' in St Andrew's Church, Dunedin, to a congregation that included many of the town's leading citizens. No reporters were present but the gist of what he said swept around the city the next day by word of mouth, jolted consciences around New Zealand over the following weeks, and coloured the attitude of politicians towards workers' rights for a generation.

The Presbyterian minister was devout in his belief that Christians had serious obligations towards fellow citizens as well as to God. He claimed that women were working fourteen or more hours a day as seamstresses for as little as two shillings. He urged a campaign against what was then called the 'sweating' of the poor. The working classes did not go to church, he said, because 'capitalists prayed for them on Sundays and preyed on them for the other six days of the week'.

The controversy that erupted in Dunedin by word of mouth after his sermon was between those in the church who believed their leaders should worry about Christian souls and not the body politic and those who believed the church had social responsibilities. The *Otago Daily Times* assigned a senior reporter to investigate the allegations, and he found it was one thing to denounce the preacher but quite another to dispose of his claims.

A small man with a slight speech impediment but mentally tough, Waddell was unfazed by the controversy, and continued his sermons on social injustice over following Sundays. They were not simply moral homilies. He offered anecdotes on hours, pay and working conditions among seamstresses. He told, for example, of one woman who worked from nine in the morning to seven in the evening making a gross of oatmeal bags for a daily pay of eight pence.

Although the longest economic depression in New Zealand's history dragged on through the 1880s, most people were unaware of the extent of the oppression of the women and, alerted by Waddell, were fearful that the sweatshops of the old world were taking hold in the new. A group composed of what one commentator described as 'old men' opposed further action by the church, but the Presbyterian synod passed a motion that it 'deplores the existence of the sweating system in the Colony, and instructs the ministers and the office-bearers to discourage it by every means in their power, and enjoins all to bear each other's burdens and so fulfil the law of Christ'.

Public opinion was deeply stirred by the issue and the Presbyterian minister from Dunedin became a national hero. When a Tailoresses' Union was formed, the first women's union in the country, he was elected its first president (just for three months, as a gesture).

The *Otago Daily Times* published a pamphlet, *The Sweating System*, followed by a large public meeting chaired by MP W Downie Stewart, father of a later Minister of Finance. Waddell reported at length on the failure of a negotiating group to persuade warehouse managers to agree on paying the seamstresses at a fair rate.

The government accepted a resolution by the meeting to set up a Royal Commission on industrial conditions, of which Waddell was a member. The commission's findings led to legislative action on the way factories operated and enforced a system of inspection. These findings also gave powerful impetus to the Industrial Conciliation and Arbitration Act, the most far-reaching piece of industrial legislation of its time, which was passed in 1894.

The Irish-born Waddell was well read, an elegant writer and a literary critic of some note but, more than anything else, a moralist. In its obituary, the *Otago Daily Times* said his standard of judgement as a critic was 'distinctly more ethical than literary'. His national fame hung on that blistering sermon delivered in St Andrew's Church. He lived through to the middle of the economic depression of the 1930s and remained all that time a working-class hero, deeply admired in Dunedin for his compassion towards the disadvantaged.

Twenty-four

TEMPTRESSES AND THE CASE FOR UGLY MPs

Whatever newspapers expected on the day New Zealand women first went to vote, what they got was a calm and orderly procession to the polls, mostly in the morning. William Pember Reeves wrote that as the result of an 'amicable arrangement', women were 'allowed, in the cities, to have certain booths pretty much to themselves until noon'.

Premier Richard Seddon said later: 'By granting the franchise to women, Parliament plunged into an abyss of unknown depth.' And commentators were unsure what would happen when women went to the booths and, later, if their effect on the result would become clear. A surprisingly high seventy-eight per cent of 140,000 eligible women had registered.

And so on a polling day in November 1893 that was bright and sunny through most of the country, only ten weeks after the Electoral Act gave them the vote, 'women tidied up the house,' said one reporter, 'put on their best clothes and walked to the booths' – more than 90,000 of them.

'All things were done in courtesy and order without rudeness, hustling or hysteria,' wrote Reeves, as though surprised. He had opposed, at first anyway, a blanket franchise for women, perhaps because he was fighting to retain his Christchurch City seat. 'Good-natured neighbours took it in turns to look after each other's children while the voting was being done ... In the towns [after the polls closed], crowds of men and women stood patiently in the streets from about nine o'clock onwards, waiting to see the results not only in their own district but of the colony's elections.

'The order kept by these thousands of full-fledged citizens was astonishing. They talked, laughed and chaffed each other, and boys ran about shouting. There was no drunkenness, no brutality. Each party received verdicts, as they were posted up, with groans or acclamation. The interest was the keenest, but, as there was no irresponsible, voteless crowd merely bent on horseplay, there was no rowdyism.'

The myth that the world-first vote for women arose spontaneously from the reforming zeal of the Ballance–Seddon Liberal Party in the early 1890s is an enduring one. In fact, the seeds of change had arrived in New Zealand fifty years before and, although the drive for extending the franchise to women was only fitfully expressed in Parliament, it had among its proselytisers almost as many conservatives as liberals. The campaign was inextricably tied up with the temperance movement, the rationale being that if women were given the vote they would mostly support Prohibition because they were seen as the prime victims of the heavy-drinking male culture of the day. That turned out to be mostly right.

Alfred Saunders, later Superintendent of Nelson Province and an MP from 1877 to 1881 and from 1889 to 1896, first publicly mooted giving women the vote soon after his arrival in New Zealand in 1843 from England. On his way out to Nelson, aboard the *Fifeshire*, he had formed a temperance society, which he claimed was New Zealand's first, launching a crusade he continued loudly throughout his life. His pursuit of votes for women was a concomitant of that crusade and he never let up, for fifty years until it became law. It was said of him by historian Bernard Foster: 'In the cut and thrust of parliamentary debate, Saunders preferred the mace to the rapier.'

Among the supporters of the cause was a Mrs Muller who wrote anonymous articles in a Nelson newspaper, despite the opposition of her husband, Resident Magistrate for Wairau, who not only opposed women voting but objected to his wife taking part in the campaign. She remained adamant, however, and worked hard for many years for reforms on behalf of women.

Some conservative politicians who also pushed the cause were four-times Premier William Fox, and John Hall, Premier from 1879 to 1882; when the law was finally passed in 1893 a number of politicians considered conservative supported it. According to James Drummond, a journalist of the time and, later, Seddon's biographer, 'Several of the strongest supporters of the movement in favour of extending the franchise were Conservatives, who believed that a vast majority of the women of the colony would vote on the side that was conservative in instinct, and Liberal leaders feared that many women would be captured by the social positions of leading Conservatives'. So the belief among Conservatives that women would vote for Prohibition and against liberal ideals pulled from them a formidable core of votes.

In 1877, an Auckland MP, Dr James Wallis, had moved 'That, in the opinion of this House, the electoral disabilities of women should be entirely removed, and that the same political rights and privileges should be granted to women as to men.' By that time women ratepayers could vote in municipal elections and for education boards, and hold office.

John Ballance had long been forcefully behind women's franchise. Seddon was known to be lukewarm on the issue and believed women should be homemakers but did support it when it gained full political momentum. Canterbury-born Fabian Socialist William Pember Reeves, a man with the disposition of a patrician, described himself as 'a half-loaf man'. He thought the vote should be given to women 'gradually, cautiously, and tentatively', starting with those who had passed the university matriculation exam. He went so far as to suggest women had not demanded the vote and many would be more unfit than were large numbers of the electors in whose hands it had been placed already.

Ballance nearly pulled off a spectacular coup in 1879 by getting the word 'person' substituted for 'man' in a Qualifications of Electors Bill, which would have given women the right to vote if they qualified not only according to the property qualifications of the time but with a residential qualification not needed by men. Some supporters decided it would have been the thin end of the wedge but others, more ardent, refused to compromise. The move only narrowly failed.

In 1881, Dr Wallis introduced the first Women's Franchise Bill. It died early, a victim of ridicule and boorish invective, and the issue lay dormant for five years. It was resuscitated by the most unlikely proponent – the conservative Julius Vogel, who re-entered politics on returning from a few years in England. Again it was countered by its entrenched opponents with ridicule and persiflage but Vogel was not a man to be trifled with. Drummond wrote of his speech: 'It was a calm array of solid arguments with very little appeal to sentiment, and it may be said to be one of the best attempts made in the colony to place the case for the women clearly and forcibly before the people.'

Vogel's Bill provided also for women to be eligible to take their place in Parliament, which prompted the following speech from Wi Pere, the MP for Eastern Maori, speaking through an interpreter: 'My opinion of this measure is that if it becomes law it will be a source of trouble to this House. I think we have only to look back to the trouble that came upon Adam through his wife giving him an apple. We should bear in mind the evil that befell Samson when his locks were shorn by Delilah . . . I am afraid that if ladies were allowed seats in the House it would distract the attention of some honourable members, and they would not pay so much attention to the affairs of the colony as they would otherwise do. Although I am getting up in years I must confess that I should be affected by a weakness of that sort.

'If the honourable gentleman in charge of this Bill would introduce the clause providing that only plain women should be allowed to come into the House, I think the source of danger would be removed; but if any beautiful ladies were sent to this House I am quite sure they would lead astray the tender hearts of some honourable gentlemen, particularly the elder members of the House. I say in conclusion that if attractive ladies are allowed to come into this House I am quite certain my own wife will never consent to my returning here.'

Satire? Apparently not. He voted against the Bill.

The second reading passed by forty-one to twenty-two. An attempt was made to limit the vote to only those women who owned property, but the Bill's supporters refused to compromise and for that and other reasons it died by only two votes.

It was then, in 1887, that the talented organiser and redoubtable confronter Kate Sheppard was appointed superintendent of the New Zealand Christian Temperance Union. She rallied the support of the many sympathetic MPs and by 1891 when Parliament met, John Hall was ready with a petition containing 10,000 women's signatures in favour of the cause. First, he presented several small lists, and two opponents scornfully remarked that so few women were interested. He then presented his main petition, a scroll more than fifty metres long. One end was grasped by another MP who pulled it after him to the furthest end of the chamber.

The House of Representatives was now in favour but the Legislative Council blocked it and it was shelved for another two years. Then, in 1893, Hall was ready with a petition carrying the names of 31,000 women, compiled by Kate Sheppard and her indefatigable associates. The Christian Women's Temperance Union had set up franchise groups throughout the country. The Legislative Council passed the Bill and it needed only vice-regal assent to become law. But Parliamentary opponents fought on, writing to the Governor, the Earl of Glasgow, urging him to withhold his signature on the grounds that they believed the majority was against it and electors had had no opportunity to express their opinions on the subject.

Sheppard then wrote her own letter to the Governor in which she forthrightly pointed out that immediately before the previous general election, John Hall had withdrawn his franchise Bill on the ground that the question had not gone before the country. She said the issue had been a major one during the election campaign and the electorate had returned a large majority of MPs who were known to favour the reform. This was reflected in the size of the number who voted for the proposed law.

The Governor signed the Bill and then, in a gesture of admiration, presented the pen he used to Mrs Sheppard.

So women's franchise did not suddenly take off with the Liberal Party's explosion of radical legislation in the 1890s but had been revving up on the runway of Parliamentary democracy in New Zealand for fifty years.

Twenty-five

THE NEMESIS OF DUMMYISM

On 21 June 1901, the Duke of York's train from Christchurch to Dunedin ceased its royal progress for a short while at Shag Point, a few kilometres north-east of Palmerston. A tall, pale man, his clothes hanging on his big frame, stood on the platform, surrounded by his family. He was helped unsteadily into the Duke's carriage, where he was pronounced a Knight Commander of the Order of St Michael and St George (KCMG). When the train continued on its journey through that cold southern day, Sir John McKenzie – the man who had effectively ended any chance that New Zealand would become a country of vast estates owned by companies or a rural aristocracy – went home to die of the cancer that had been eating away at him for two years. It took barely another six months.

Forty-one years and one month before that day on the ducal train at Shag Point, McKenzie had left Scotland for two good reasons: to escape a scandal and because he

145

was the second oldest of ten children of a tenant farmer and had to make his own way in the world. His family was devoutly Presbyterian, walking many kilometres to kirk on Sundays, but John fathered an illegitimate son to a woman who refused to marry him. He gave the boy his name to mitigate the stigma of illegitimacy and less than a year later, in 1860, married Ann Munro, six years older than him, and left for the Scottish settlement of Dunedin.

McKenzie was a humourless, hypersensitive man with a frightening temper, whose first language was Gaelic and whose education at home was barely adequate for public life. The Bible, which he read avidly, and many of his other books were in Gaelic, but he worked hard for years at his English. When he gained a seat in Parliament he would practise speeches at home, standing at one end of a room and orating to his family at the other. But if his classically educated (usually landowning) opponents in Parliament taunted him with Greek or Latin jibes he would lapse in anger into Gaelic.

His other interest was Scottish history, as though he wanted to remind himself what not to do, because McKenzie's career and his fame rested on his obsession: landlordism. He would brook no opposition when it came to breaking up large estates or allowing absentee landlordism. As he grew up, the Highland clearances were under way in Scotland. The Duke of Sutherland, later followed by other landlords, heartlessly evicted tenant farmers and merged their small holdings into large sheep farms. The farmers were left with nothing and almost nowhere to go. In a public speech he repeated many times McKenzie said: 'I have seen the poor people evicted from their homes in a most cruel manner, and unable to get a place for their feet to stand on except they went to the cemeteries. They were not even allowed to camp on the King's highway. The only place in the world where they could go and rest themselves without being put in jail was among the dead in the cemeteries.' Scottish histories of the time confirm that no other tenants would help the dispossessed in case they were similarly evicted, so many of the dispossessed camped in country churchyards as the only place of refuge.

McKenzie was no radical on any issue except land tenure and he caught a tide of liberal opinion in his time that favoured the nationalisation of land and leases to farmers on condition that they lived and worked on the farms. The movement had been embraced by the future Prime Minister John Ballance and leading Liberal Robert Stout, who was more doctrinaire and formed a Land Nationalisation Society in Dunedin. McKenzie also fought for access to the countryside by the common people through the Queen's chain, and provided scientific resources to support farmers through the Department of Agriculture. But a man who stoutly opposed women's suffrage, favoured capital punishment and wanted Maori land titles individualised and made available for sale hardly ever spoke on issues other than land tenure and farming. Yet he rose to be Seddon's right-hand man and led the government in the Premier's absence.

The nationalisation and leasehold movement was never going to win in New Zealand or any country with the British cultural tradition of land ownership. But McKenzie's achievement was this. While he believed that freehold land was, well, immoral, the bedrock of his belief was the concept of the family farm; so that the man who worked the soil and managed the stock should not be paying rent to a land company or a wealthy man living in town on unearned income. Consequently, as Minister of Lands in the Liberal government during the 1890s, he moved from coercion to compulsion to forcibly break up the big estates against the most tenacious and cunning opposition, backed, as it was, by the power of money.

Despite the land-reforming zeal of some Liberals, the policies McKenzie adopted were pragmatic rather than ideological and they worked wonderfully well. More than half a million hectares of land were opened up for about 7000 farmers, and the result was increased and diversified primary production. But the leasehold movement lasted for many years with gradually declining support. Early in his political career, a United Party Prime Minister (1930–35) George Forbes had been an avid advocate of leasehold, but his vision faded, became fainter and fainter, the longer he stayed in politics.

History demonstrates time and again that working the land changes men into political conservatives. And so, through historical irony, the very families radical Liberal Party policies had placed on the land began to turn against their former benefactors and vote for more conservative opposition parties, leading to the William Massey administration in 1911.

In his early days in Cabinet, on the way to fool-proof legislation which finally had the desired effect, McKenzie and the Ministers of Lands before him, William Rolleston and Ballance, faced many rorts by the rich, including 'dummyism', which worked like this. A company or wealthy family would 'borrow' names to buy more than the legal limit of land. The people, some of them from old people's homes, had their names used on titles, and were often moved into houses on the property to live rent-free. They happily signed promissory notes for the value of the property so they couldn't later claim the land was theirs. Thus station owners added thousands of acres on which to run their sheep. The ruse was uncovered during inquiries into land ownership after the government became aware of abuses.

When John McKenzie first arrived in New Zealand he worked as a shepherd and by dint of intelligence and hard work gradually earned enough to buy his own property near Palmerston. On the top of the hill at Puketapu, above Palmerston, where he was buried, a cairn has been erected in his memory. From there, you can see flourishing family farms that might have been just part of a huge sheep station had it not been for McKenzie.

He was not an attractive man – one writer described his 'little deep-set eyes' – but he was implacably honest among many who were not so straight in the Liberal government he loyally supported. He was self-righteously immovable in his opposition to landlordism and more than any other politician of his time constructed the conditions for the family farm on which the economy of New Zealand was based for most of the twentieth century.

Another McKenzie legacy was a huge family. He had only six children himself but his father had had ten children by John's mother and five more to a second wife when he remarried at age sixty-five after his wife's death. Many of his brothers and half-brothers followed John's migrant trail. By 1898, more than eighty descendants of his father were living in New Zealand.

Twenty-six

THE DOG TAX REBELLION –
THE LAST MAORI ARMED UPRISING

In the winter of 1898, seventy armed Maori from the Mahurehure marae lay along the crest of Waima Hill in the Hokianga ready to ambush a military force on the way to subdue and arrest them.

Rawene was evacuated by the government steamer *Hinemoa*. Two naval vessels arrived: one carried thirty soldiers and a machine-gun; the other patrolled Hokianga Harbour day and night, sweeping the surrounding hills with a searchlight after dark. And all because local Maori refused to pay the Hokianga County Council's annual dog registration tax of two shillings and sixpence for each animal.

Maori had objected to the tax since its inception in the early years of the decade and in 1898 decided not to pay it. They had stockpiled arms and ammunition and when some of the hapu were summonsed for non-payment, Waima chief Hone Toia led a protest in the streets of Rawene. He and his followers brandished their guns at the watching policeman. One commentator noted that it was a difficult time for Hokianga Maori, many of whom had lost their land and become tenants, thus doubly bearing the brunt of colonisation.

It was said of Prime Minister Richard John Seddon by his biographer RM Burdon that he 'habitually reacted violently to the faintest threat of violence' and he did on this occasion. Maori MP Hone Heke Rankin rushed to the scene and then urged Seddon to restrain his hand while he acted as peacemaker. Rankin had played the role before because he was not without mana among Maori. He was a grand-nephew of myth-maker Hone Heke, who cut down the flagstaff at Kororareka, and great-grand-nephew of another legendary warrior, Hongi Hika.

The Maori had protested about the tax more than once and Seddon, who had visited the Hokianga during a national tour in 1894 to investigate Maori grievances, remembered complaints he had received both from Maori at the tax and from Pakeha at Maori protests against it. So he dispatched the *Hinemoa*, the *Gairlock*, with the soldiers aboard, and the armed vessel, the *Torch*. When Rankin asked for patience, Seddon bluntly refused. When Rankin, more desperately, again sought time, Seddon brushed the request aside and demanded unconditional surrender by the rebels.

Working under the pressure this imposed, Rankin spent a day and a night with the Mahurehure hapu, persuading Hone Toia and his men to return to the marae and surrender rather than commit an act of armed rebellion when the army detachment arrived, with all the dire consequences of such an action for local Maori.

Rankin stayed on in the area for several weeks calming the situation.

Toia and twelve other men from Mahurehure were arrested and spent two years in prison. And the only thanks Rankin got was a deduction from his parliamentary honorarium for the time he spent peacemaking in Hokianga.

Footnote: Elected MP for Northern Maori in 1893, Rankin had once before defused potential armed rebellion. In 1895, government surveyors had appeared at Ruatoki in the Ureweras and the local Maori knew from experience that once surveyors appeared it wasn't long before they would lose their land. They obstructed and threatened the visitors. Seddon immediately dispatched police and army detachments. Rankin managed to broker a peace while Seddon was accusing him of fomenting disorder. By the time the troops arrived, they were met peaceably by the local chiefs and allowed to proceed.

Twenty-seven

THE TYPICAL ABOUT-FACE IDEOLOGUE

The ideologue has a singular cast of mind, one that needs bold rules and eschews nuances. Abundant examples exist of those who, devout in proselytising for one belief system, undergo an epiphany, and then reach in sudden disillusionment for a diametrically opposed but equally rigid creed. It occasions no surprise to the worldly when a devotee of the extreme Left suffers a dramatic change of mind and joins the extreme Right.

One of these about-face believers was William Lane, editorial writer and then editor of the *New Zealand Herald* from 1900 until 1917. He was a man who held two diametrically different views of the world in his lifetime. First, he was a rabble-rousing radical republican and Communist, and secondly, he was the most fervidly reactionary jingoistic journalist in New Zealand during the run-up to the First World War. He remained a supporter of that great disaster until he died in 1917, long after many observers had become disenchanted with the pointless carnage.

A small, limping man with large, short-sighted blue eyes, Lane spoke and wrote skilfully and with the kind of persuasive intensity that enabled him, in 1893, to recruit 220 Australians and New Zealanders to join him in establishing 'New Australia', a commune in, of all places, Paraguay, where they would 'prove to the world that Communism is a practicable system of society'. The group assembled enough money to buy a ship and off they went to land they had bought in the former Spanish colony in South America.

Lane was born in Bristol, England, in 1861. Lame from birth, he left school at fourteen, worked as a clerk, emigrated to Canada at fifteen and moved on to the United States, working on a number of newspapers, first as a compositor and then as a reporter. In Michigan, in 1883, he married Annie Macguire, and they emigrated to Brisbane where he became a radical socialist, conditioned by his working-class origins. His aim was 'to idealise Labour, to conquer want, and hate and greed, and vice, and establish peace on earth and goodwill towards men'.

He became editor of *The Worker*, the first trade-union newspaper in Australia, whose masthead included 'Socialism in Our Time'. He became a powerful voice for the Labour movement and wrote a novel, *The Workingman's Paradise*, whose heroes were working-class mates. This rose-tinted view of mateship led him next to bucolic, utopian socialism, an ideal that had many proponents in the Western world as working people tried to cope with the crowding, the grime and the long working hours of the Industrial Revolution. Lane's powers of persuasion made many men and women follow his dream of a democratic, communal life.

Australia was suffering serious economic problems at the time as shearers and farmers faced off in a strike that lasted two years; and New Zealand was in the grip of what was the longest economic depression in the country's history. Declining wool prices had hit both countries hard, but the class war broke into open conflict in Australia, with woolsheds burnt down and shots fired lethally in anger. The language of workers' pamphlets conveys the political tenor of the time. For example: 'The Tree of Liberty only bears fruit when manured with the bones of the fat usurers and insolent despots.' And worse, a pamphlet urged men 'to study the science of death, use bullets, steel . . . kerosene . . . poison, blasting powder . . . You must steal like Spartans, think like heroes, lie like hell.'

It was in this environment that Lane left *The Worker*, helped form the New Australia Co-operative Settlement Association and began plans for a utopia, a new Canaan, in some other country. He despaired of the future of the working class in Australia and saw hope only in leaving it. Those who joined him had to commit all their worldly wealth, with a minimum of £60, and they had to be racially pure Caucasians.

Argentina was examined but discarded as a prospect. When the investigating party (not including Lane) went to Paraguay, it found a number of English already settled there. President Gonzales welcomed the utopian plan, offering protection from interference by provincial officials. The affairs of the colony would be subject only to the national government. The Paraguayan Foreign Minister accompanied the Australian party to land thought desirable for settlement, and he regaled them with stories of longstanding socialist communities. The British Legation in Buenos Aires waxed positive about the land the Paraguayan government offered on very generous terms. So the New Australia association bought the land and decided this land-locked South American country would become their new utopian home.

The project was initially disastrous. New Australia took only a year to fall apart. Leadership became a problem as Lane suspended their constitution, high-handedly expelling members for drunkenness and other 'offences'. Dissension became persistent. Among those who seceded from the settlement, some were transported to the Gonzalez Colony, established on the principle not of common ownership but on the basis of allocated private allotments to members. Some returned home to Australia in 1895. Lane, his family and about sixty others left the main settlement to found another commune called Cosme. Lane went to England and recruited new members from there, building up the numbers to eighty. Then, six years after their arrival, Lane and his family suddenly left the commune and Paraguay, and briefly revisited Australia where he returned to *The Worker*, before moving to New Zealand.

His disenchantment with socialism was swift and dramatic. In 1900 he joined the *New Zealand Herald* and quickly established himself as a journalist with an entirely different persona from the one William Lane wore in his former life in Australia and Paraguay. The only consistent belief that survived the transformation

from devout, atheistic communist into outspoken supporter of unbridled, jingoistic capitalism and orthodox
Christianity derived from a stain in his mind about race.
The British, he had never doubted, were superior to all
other people, and blacks and Asians inherently inferior.
He adopted wholeheartedly the Yellow Peril, the Russian
Scare and nasty German militarism mentality and was
instrumental in the formation of the rabidly imperial-
ist National Defence League of New Zealand, which
drummed up such support in the Auckland region
for compulsory military training that the government
acquiesced and introduced it in 1909.

Lane's pen-name was Tohunga and his columns
became a must-read for Establishment New Zealand.
Several years before war broke out, but seemed imminent, he wrote: 'All the tales of scarlet battlefields and
moan-echoing hospital wards never helped for peace yet
and never will. For pain is, after all, only the background
for pleasure. Or it may be that pain is, in itself, as much
craved for by normal natures as pleasure, and that hap-
piness is only found in a judicious mixture of both. At
any rate there can be little doubt that pleasure and pain
are experienced in the highest degree only in the more
developed and sensitive races. What we term "native"
races certainly feel little of either, as we understand
feeling . . .'

With this overtone of sadomasochism, he became an
indefatigable promoter of the rightness of the war, of
the glory of dying for one's country and the necessity
of suppressing any dissent from overt patriotism. Not
long before he died suddenly in 1917, Tohunga wrote:
'Righteous war with its appeal to all that is highest and

noblest in the human heart, with its inexorable demand for self-sacrifice, with its frank presentation of duty-doing, with its stern teaching that the worthy man must offer his life if Humanity is to save its soul is profoundly affecting the thoughts of men and women upon living and after-living.' He ended with: 'And who will doubt that all who toiled and sought or fought and died to make the world more free and humanity better will reap together in the after-living the harvest of their sowing.'

Lane's unequivocal nationalism and intolerance of beliefs he had once deeply held himself and had power-fully propagated had a significant effect on New Zealand opinion in the early years of the twentieth century, years which were, in the main, prosperous. His Tohunga arti-cles were briskly written, exemplary forms of journalism, so admired for their content that many were reproduced in book form.

He was survived by his wife and six of their eleven children.

Footnote: Although many of the Australian and New Zealand settlers returned from Paraguay, most stayed on. As the New Australia colony dropped its communal living and began to prosper, some of those who had left in disillusionment went back to Paraguay; so a substantial number of Paraguayans today are descendants of those who went there in hope, sank into despair and finally emerged as moderately prosperous.

Twenty-eight

AN EMISSARY FROM A SUPERIOR RACE

On a Sunday evening in September 1905, Lionel Terry, a much-travelled Englishman poisoned by racial obsessions, stepped up to a crippled Chinese tottering along Wellington's Haining Street, and murdered him. A Chinese man over the road heard the first shot and saw the second one fired, both to the back of Joe Kum Yung's head from close range.

Haining Street was a Chinese enclave and as the old man's neighbours crowded onto the street, Terry strode off to the Lambton Quay Police Station and asked to see an officer. The constable at the desk told him no one was available. They had all sped to Haining Street in response to a call about the shooting.

Terry then went back to the Club Hotel where he was living and where other guests considered him an engaging man – 190 centimetres tall, handsome and an entertaining conversationalist. After supper, he auctioned his handmade walking stick because, he said, he would not need it any more. Next morning at half-past nine, he returned to the police station, told the watch-keeper he had killed the Chinese man and put his revolver on the counter. Three of the five chambers were still loaded.

Terry had made no attempt to hide his obsessive hatred of Chinese. He had written a book called *The Shadow*, making a case against alien immigration, had lobbied at least one MP to have Chinese immigration stopped and those already here repatriated, and would make his views known in conversation to anyone who would listen. As social obsessions usually do, Terry's insane beliefs had grown from a common political undercurrent. During the Victorian Age even intelligent, educated people clung to some sad old prejudices and invented some strange new ones, such as eugenics which favoured sterilising the 'unfit' in society, wanting to usurp the role of nature to ensure the survival of the fittest. Darwinism was bent into a theory that some races had advanced higher in evolutionary development than others. The British believed this in a somewhat tepid way to justify colonialism as an attempt to civilise what they considered lesser cultures.

New Zealanders were not immune to these theories, and their attitude towards some races became paranoiac because of their geographic isolation – a small, under-populated British country, far away from Mother England, sitting at the bottom of a Pacific rimmed with millions of 'Asiatics'. They had been suspicious of the French, especially during intermittent wars with Britain, but they reserved their special fears for highly populated, nearer nations about which they knew little but which were so populous they loomed as potential invaders.

The first and most consistent threat was perceived as

coming from China. Chinese migrated to New Zealand in some numbers during the Central Otago gold rush (about 4000 had come by the late 1860s), where they were allowed to work over the tailings after European miners had moved on. So frightened were governments of the time that the Chinese would come in by the thousands and swamp the local population that they imposed restrictions such as language tests and a poll tax to keep the numbers down.

The different living styles of the Chinese also worried New Zealanders, and this and their frequent language difficulties meant they lived in enclaves, mostly without female companions. And yet those who mixed closely with them even in the early days found little to be concerned about. Alexander Bathgate was a Scot who arrived in Otago in 1862 and served as a banker at the Central Otago diggings before practising as a lawyer in Dunedin. He wrote in *Colonial Experiences*, published in Glasgow in 1874: 'At the time the Chinese began to visit Otago, numbers of men were out of employment, and there were frequent murmurs from the working-classes. The strangers did not, however, interfere with the labour market, but at once adopted gold mining as their pursuit, and plodded patiently at it, a course which was open to any European unemployed . . .

'Since their arrival, they have quite lived down the evil reports circulated before their coming; and, though one or two have figured in the criminal calendar, they have on the whole proved themselves peaceable and orderly citizens . . .

'Taken as a whole, the heathen Chinese are a very hard-working, industrious, steady people, generally of a light-hearted, merry disposition, and, though wearing usually solemn countenances, are easily amused . . .'

Bathgate reflected a decent and generous attitude that was widespread in the Dunedin of those days and became a characteristic of New Zealand culture since. He noted that there was only one incident in Otago of the sort of violence against the Chinese that occurred on a large scale at the Victorian diggings: thirteen months after Terry killed Joe Kum Yung in Wellington, a Dunedin fish hawker, Lin Foon, fired two shots at and wounded a tramway worker, Peter McKewan. The Supreme Court jury found Lin Foon guilty but recommended mercy. The judge released him on a good-behaviour bond, taking into account evidence that the defendant was a gentle and inoffensive person who had been harassed and was defending himself.

However, something Bathgate wrote gently expressed the fears of those in other parts of the country who did not know the Chinese: 'The yellow men are fast spreading themselves all over the world; and they appear destined to play a not unimportant part in its future history. Possessing all the powers of the Anglo-Saxon race, of adapting themselves to various climates, they excel the Saxon in their powers of enduring heat; and I doubt not their race will one day predominate in many of the hotter parts of the Australian continent.'

Some populist politicians and newspapers tapped into the deep-seated fears of what was called the Yellow Peril. In a moment of mad, chauvinistic racism, Prime Minister Richard Seddon famously told Queen Maketu in Rarotonga that Cook Islanders would do better to have the bubonic plague than Chinese immigrants.

The Auckland-based National Defence League of New Zealand recruited 6600 members, advocating compulsory military training to be prepared against 'the unnameable horrors of Asiatic hordes'.

So Lionel Terry's murderous gesture against miscegenation was an insane extension of some attitudes that were far from unpopular.

Terry defended himself at his trial, objecting to the word 'guilty'. He said his action was right and justified, which the judge inferred was a 'not guilty' plea. He made a long speech to the jury in which he said his act was a gesture to gain attention to his cause, that he had no personal enmity to the dead man, indeed had chosen him because he was old and crippled and, therefore, a burden to himself. Reports said that Terry was rational, dignified and skilful in his own defence.

The jury found him guilty with a recommendation for mercy justified by his 'suffering mentally from a craze caused by his intense hatred towards the mixing of British and alien races'.

New Zealand's most famous woman physician of her time, Dr Doris Gordon, wrote about Terry in the first volume of her autobiography, *Backblocks Baby Doctor*. As a young graduate of Otago Medical School in 1915, she visited Seacliff where the superintendent, Dr Truby King, chaired a lecture he allowed Terry to give. By the time the inmate, who had a 'wonderful physique and brilliant brain', had finished, 'most of the hypnotised students were wondering who should be labelled lunatic and who custodian'.

Terry was thirty-eight at the time of the murder and eighty-five when he died, still in custody at Seacliff, in 1952; by which time New Zealand had survived an attempt at Japanese imperialism and was on the way towards accepting its place in the Pacific.

Twenty-nine

THE GREAT WHITE FLEET ARRIVES

The visit to New Zealand of the United States Navy's White Squadron in 1908 is barely a footnote to history today, but it had the most extraordinary effect on the country at the time. When the battleships steamed into the Waitemata Harbour on 9 August at the beginning of what was called 'Fleet Week' (9–15 August), city librarian and historian John Barr claimed 100,000 people 'utilised every vantage point on the harbour front'. Not bad when you consider the population of Auckland City at the time was less than 40,000.

Even the extreme remoteness of New Zealand at the time hardly explains an air of mad jubilation that took over the whole country. The Chief Justice, Sir Robert Stout, descended to abject hyperbole when he began the foreword to an *Auckland Weekly News* feature with: 'The visit to New Zealand of some of the war vessels of the United States is as great an event in our history as was the first visit of the intrepid voyager Captain Cook.'

The Prime Minister, Joseph Ward, never managed to distort reality that much, but he demeaned himself and New Zealand in the most extraordinary manner. He sent a message to the fleet commander, Rear-Admiral Charles S Sperry: 'We scarce can make our welcome give expression to our hearts, which felt as your fleet swung majestically to anchorage that they were the noble war-ships of our kindred and our pride in their arrival was greater than your own.'

Ward wrote an introduction to a special 270-page, hardcover book entitled *Souvenir of the Visit of the American Fleet to Auckland, New Zealand*, published by the government and written by the country's top journal-ist of the day, James Cowan. Ward said: 'Today there rises in our breasts a special pride in our old Anglo-Saxon race, for are you not a branch of that great tree which has spread from clime to clime to raise the level of the world's civilisation?'

Both Stout and Ward lamented at length that the War of Independence had severed the ties between Britain and the US. Ward eulogised President Theodore Roosevelt as 'cherished, honoured and revered' in New Zealand. He concluded: 'It is all these thoughts and feelings stirring in our hearts today that lift our welcome above any mere international courtesy. Our hearts go out to you – our hands grasp yours as brothers, friends, and fellow sailors.'

The 'Great White Fleet', as it was tagged, consisted of sixteen battleships, including Perry's flagship, the *Connecticut*, with attendant auxiliaries and colliers. The ships' complements totalled 12,000. John Barr said: 'The City was decorated in the most elaborate manner, electricity being used for the first time in the illuminations, which were a feature of the nocturnal displays . . .'

Fleet Week was 'a week of festivities, the like of which the city had never previously indulged in'. Barr said these took the form of 'banquets, receptions on land and aboard the ships of the fleet, reviews, race meetings and sports, both general and aquatic. Public and private or-ganisations vied with each other in the entertainment of both officers and men'.

Naval visits always attracted great interest among Aucklanders. Royal Navy ships had called regularly since the earliest days of the colony, Australian warships visited occasionally and vessels from France, Russia, Germany and Japan had called over the years – some more welcome than others. When the Royal Navy battle-cruiser HMS *New Zealand* visited in April 1913, under the shadow of war, nearly 95,000 New Zealanders visited her.

But nothing matched the public jubilation of the Americans' visit, nor the cringing adulation of politi-cians. Perhaps the biggest clue to this comes from the second paragraph of Stout's foreword in which he said: 'The trend of empire, it has been said, is westward, and it is no longer who is to rule the Mediterranean or to be master of the Atlantic, but who is to dominate the Pacific. There are at least seven Powers spoken of in the Pacific – Russia, Japan, China, France, Germany, Britain, and the United States. Is the last named to be the first power and influence?' It proved a pertinent question, garbed as it was in hope.

Stout also went on and on about French and German intrusions into the Pacific and about lost British oppor-tunities in Tahiti, Samoa, Easter Island and other Pacific countries that had been annexed by foreign nations. He accused British statesmen of being 'deplorably short-sighted' on 'Pacific questions' over the years, adding: 'With no harbour in the eastern Pacific, how can the British hope to be the main power in the Pacific . . . ?'

This was about a decade after the Russian Scare reached fever pitch, and a year after Lionel Terry murdered Joe Kum Yung. Mother England was a long way away, with conflicting colonial interests around the world. Obviously, the sense that the United States was emerging as the best hope for New Zealand protection was behind the excesses of leaders, such as Ward's peroration: 'The armaments of America, and above all, her navy, are but majestic instruments for working out the aims of higher civilization. Your fleet stands for peace, not war – for justice, not aggression – for freedom not tyranny.'

Thirty

PARIS? POOF! RESTAURANTS ARE SHABBY AND THE SEINE A DIRTY DITCH

Andrew William Rutherford, who owned 15,000 hectares of sheep station in Canterbury, a colonial born and bred, looked around with disdain on his first morning in the City of Light. 'The streets of Paris are not equal to those of any of our chief cities,' he wrote back to the *Press*. 'The restaurants, of which one hears so much, are mean, shabby affairs, half on the footpath and half inside. I allude to the respectable ones. It is a matter of common knowledge that the swell restaurants are the haunts of gilded vice. There are none of them on the footpath. Quite a large revenue is derived by municipalities in France from the footpaths. The restaurants are the best customers. Sometimes they take possession of two-thirds ... In some of the narrow streets, with footpaths four feet wide, the whole width is taken up, and the pedestrian is compelled to step off into the street ...

'I may interpolate that the Seine, like the Thames, within its city boundaries, is just a dirty ditch – neither of them to be compared to the Wanganui, the Brisbane, or even the Waikato.' Yes, Rutherford was less than enchanted by Paris. He was born in New South Wales but he had built up a large station in the Amuri district and established a reputation as a New Zealand premier breeder of merinos. He was the Liberal Member of Parliament for Hurunui for six years until he retired from the House in 1908. At age sixty-eight, in 1910, he went on a world tour with his wife and three unmarried daughters. (When they married in 1873, Rutherford was thirty-one and his wife fifteen.)

New Zealand Pakeha were probably more isolated from the world in the first decade of the twentieth century than they had been for forty or more years. The huge majority of those born here could not afford the long and expensive journey to their roots in Britain and had only the tales of their parents to colour in their impressions of the Old World. When the First World War broke out in 1914, a higher proportion of New Zealanders went overseas than from any other country, and one explanation is that it was the only way they would ever get to travel to Europe.

So when Rutherford went on his travels, he arranged for the *Press* to take his articles, which were later collected in a book called *The Impressions of a Pastoralist on Tour*, published by Whitcombe and Tombs in 1911. It makes hilarious reading nowadays. One hundred and sixty centimetres tall, robustly built and famously cheerful, Rutherford suffered not at all from cultural cringe. He compared European countries with New Zealand and Australia, almost always to the extreme disadvantage of the foreigners. The French reputation for a gay and civilised life was the one he obviously thought most inflated:

'I had been under the illusion that the Parisians, both sexes, were a gay people, gaily dressed. Such is far from the case. Most of them look dowdy – scarcely a top hat or frock coat to be seen. I was told that there is display about midnight in the fashionable restaurants. I felt sure that Paris had at some time or another done something to earn its reputation for gaiety, so I made enquiries, with this result – Paris is one of the easiest places in which to empty one's pocket, and one of the most difficult in which to earn an honest penny. It is the want of money and the difficulty of earning it, which has in late years deadened much of the extravagant gaiety which once existed. Parisians are now content to match their pleasures to their purses.

'I am fast losing illusions. I had thought that the French were smaller men than the British. Possibly they are not quite so tall – I am not certain about that – but they are stouter – would weigh out better.

'On the whole, notwithstanding the new streets, Paris gave me the impression of being in a decadent state. No city can maintain continued progress whose foundation is laid on vice . . .'

Rutherford decided 'our Maoris' could give the French lessons in good manners and courtesy. Then the famous French cuisine came under colonial scrutiny:

- 'We were prejudiced; we determined not to eat horse flesh, veal, frogs or snails, or anything of that nature. If there was a doubt concerning a *plat*, well, we passed . . . You will see alongside fair beef and mutton unmistakable horse, or it may be mule or donkey flesh.

- 'Meat is not safe in France; it may be most anything, and they have a number of messy *plats* with no particular flavour, which they gobble up – they are ugly eaters.

- 'The French are great bread eaters, and to this fact the dressmakers attribute the enormous development, especially chest development, of many of the women.

- 'In Paris, [the cheese] was vile stuff . . . Much of the wine is vile; no colonial could possibly drink it . . . The cheap wines of France are deadly rubbish. I'd join the Prohibs in preference to drinking it.'

England does better but few things come up to scratch when compared with New Zealand. Extraordinarily, as a former member of the Liberal Party which gave New Zealand women the vote, Rutherford decides that women's franchise will be the death of Britain as a world leader. He notes there are many more women than men in Britain and, therefore, 'Great Britain will be ruled by women'. To grant female franchise would accentuate Britain's military decline, he decided. 'When the enemy is at the gate, where will the women be? In hysterics, and their male supporters administering restoratives to them.'

Andrew Rutherford died in the influenza epidemic at the end of the First World War, back here in Arcady.

Thirty-one

THE CLASS WAR – ITS VICTIMS AND SURVIVORS

The Industrial Conciliation and Arbitration Act of 1894 was admired and praised in countries beyond New Zealand as the way of the future to give both workers and bosses fair treatment when their interests collided. In its variously amended forms, the Act lasted for eighty years and damped down the heat from much industrial friction. But only briefly did it placate working-class socialists, many of them recent immigrants, who saw in the power of the unions a means to modify capitalist society.

As the first decade of the new century drew on, the radical, humanitarian but essentially pragmatic government of the 1990s was becoming a memory. The nation became increasingly prosperous under Richard Seddon's Liberal administrations, but conservative farmers were burgeoning into the most powerful economic group. They provided the meat, wool and dairy produce for export to Britain by means of refrigerated shipping. They saw themselves as the only sector in the country creating wealth in an era when an economy was measured by how well-fed and clothed people were.

As the industrial chaos of 1913 began, a Wellington magazine editorial said: 'Cities don't matter tuppence. The futility of this particular city would be demonstrated in a fortnight's blockade. We don't live on asphalt and the work of all the organised unionists in one closed up city wouldn't feed one man.'

But militant unionists thought otherwise. They believed their power to disrupt production and distribution of goods and services would prove how vital to economic prosperity they were and would bring workers a greater share of the national wealth. The strongest unions were those with large memberships who, by the nature of their work, could tie up production and services, workers such as miners, watersiders and transport workers. Miners and watersiders had the added advantage of working in large numbers at relatively few workplaces and could thus be assembled quickly for mass meetings. This, and the hazards of their job in the case of the miners, encouraged solidarity and an intense male camaraderie. Many saw themselves as soldiers in the class war. Which is not to say that their causes were not very often just. The class war was a social reality for manual workers in all Western countries for 100 years from the middle of the nineteenth century as they struggled to change the low wages and often appalling working conditions that followed the Industrial Revolution.

The battlegrounds for the early twentieth-century class war in New Zealand were the mining towns of Blackball, Waihi and Huntly and the main ports of Auckland and

Wellington through which the wealth flowed in and out of the country.

In 1908 miners at Blackball decided to push for a lunch break of half an hour instead of fifteen minutes. The mine owners fired the instigators. The 120 miners struck, demanding the reinstatement of their comrades. Even though a half-hour break was standard elsewhere, the Arbitration Court ruled in favour of the employers and fined the union £75. The miners remained adamant, however, and stayed out on strike for three months. The employers then surrendered and the half-hour lunch was enjoyed by Blackball miners.

This significant victory for the union ended the conviction of many that the arbitration system was a cure for industrial unrest, and prompted the formation of a Federation of Miners with Robert Semple as president. The organisation was inspired to change its name to the New Zealand Federation of Labour a year later in a bid to widen membership and influence. Members were dubbed 'Red Feds'.

In 1909, the Waihi Miners' and Workers' Union joined the federation. Small gains in wages and conditions were immediate. Two years later the union deregistered from the Industrial Conciliation and Arbitration Act to avoid prosecution if it took direct action and struck. The Red Feds now had about a fifth of all unionists affiliated and helped manage a number of small disputes among its members with some gains; so the confidence of militant unionists was growing as the second decade of the century arrived. But then the Red Feds overplayed their hand. The Waihi mine engine drivers, more conservative members of the union, along with many people in the town, thought the Red Feds too rabidly anti-employer, and decided to secede and form the Waihi Engine Drivers and Winders' Union, and reregister with the Arbitration Court. The moment executive members of the miners' union received this news, on 12 May 1912, they called a strike. At a meeting of 700 miners later that week, the president of the Auckland General Labourers' Union, Peter Fraser, proposed the miners stay out until the engine drivers rejoined their union.

The mine owners regarded the battle as between two unions, as indeed it was, and refused at first to have any involvement apart from urging the miners back to work. On the first Saturday night, the miners were urged by Michael Joseph Savage, of the Auckland Brewery Employees' Union, to stay solid. The Federation of Labour (FOL) claimed the strike was against what it called 'sectionalism' and that the engine drivers had formed a 'scab' union. Twenty-two years later, Savage became Prime Minister and, when he died in office, was succeeded by Fraser. Others involved in the long, messy Waihi affair included Semple, Paddy Webb and William Parry, all Cabinet Ministers in the first Labour government.

Although the mine owners maintained they were victims of a union war, they were persuaded to meet FOL representatives, including Semple, Fraser, Webb and Parry, on 18 June. Semple was quoted as saying, as the meeting broke up, 'You have thrown down the gauntlet. You want a fight. Well, we are going to make it a bitter one, and bitter to the end. The gloves are off and it is going to be a knuckle fight.' Later, when he became an MP and Minister of Works, Semple was noted for his colourful and extravagant language.

Many of the miners and their families worried about their future, and Waihi's other citizens became concerned as business fell away. The strikers received money from other unions belonging to the federation but not enough to make up a full wage. Gradually tension grew, especially after July when a new, conservative Reform government won power under William Massey. The number of police in the town began to grow, some reported sixty or seventy. Miners, including their president, Parry, were charged in court with breaching the peace by harassing engine drivers, and during September more than forty were sent to Mt Eden prison.

In October, the mine reopened with new mining 'scab' staff, and a month later the trouble came to a head when a striker shot and wounded a member of the new union. Next, a constable was also shot and wounded but used his baton to beat his assailant, Fred Evans, as others in the crowd joined in. Evans later died in hospital from his injuries.

But the government won out. From the beginning of 1913, the mine slowly returned to full production with new workers.

For many years unionists regarded Waihi as a legitimate strike that was defeated only because of hated scab labour. More than thirty years later, I was in a queue for a freezing-works job in Wellington when a unionist went to the foreman and pointed out a man just ahead of me. The foreman went to the man and told him he wouldn't get a job. It was because he had been a scab at Waihi and remained blackballed by unionists.

Waihi was a serious defeat for the miners and the FOL. But worse was to come in 1913. In October, as Europe moved towards war, the miners in Huntly struck, followed by watersiders in Wellington and then Auckland. The year then became a stand-off between the industrial left and the increasingly conservative farming community, represented by Farmer Bill, Prime Minister William Massey. The government's first action was to amend the Industrial Conciliation and Arbitration Act, making it illegal for anyone or any organisation to offer help, gifts or any 'valuable thing' to strikers – legislation that echoed down the decades to the biggest industrial dispute of the century, the 1951 watersiders' stoppage.

On 22 October, 1500 waterside workers in Wellington voted to strike because the Union Steam Ship Company would not pay travelling time for shipwrights. The next day 1000 strikers picketed the wharves, bringing activity to a standstill. Three days later, the government broadened the strife into a town versus country war by re-cruiting special constables with horses to help police keep order. Farmers and their sons flocked to the banner and exacerbated rather than calmed the situation. Mounted specials, wielding long batons, rode into Auckland and Wellington, camped in army tents in public parks or were lodged in army barracks, and began patrolling with police. They were tagged 'Massey's Cossacks'.

Watersiders in Auckland and other ports came out on strike and miners and seamen joined the fray.

The first clash in Wellington saw the strikers rout the mounted specials. Massey's Cossacks retaliated later by charging a crowd in Post Office Square, but several were forced to take refuge in Whitcombe and Tombs' shop where they were defended from strikers by armed staff. On 5 November, 900 specials took part in a cavalry charge against a crowd obstructing the loading of horses for a race meeting in Christchurch. Twenty people were injured.

Protests were more subdued in Auckland where the mounted specials from the more densely farmed surrounding areas numbered 1500. As in 1951, the conservative, urban middle class may have had some sympathy with their worker neighbours but they were disturbed by the violence and fundamentally sided with the forces of law and order.

Five days before Christmas 1913, the strike was over with the unions beaten. Soon the First World War would be a distraction for all. Over the previous decade, the class war had had many victims, both economic and personal, with one man killed, dozens injured and hundreds arrested and jailed. The leaders of what had become the United Federation of Labour had learnt that the conservative New Zealander would not side with militant trade unionists, so many of the ablest of these militant unionists rose from the ashes of defeated strikes and opted for politics as the route to their vision of a socialist future.

Peter Fraser was sentenced to a year in jail in 1916 for agitating against the conscription of men for the war without 'the conscription of wealth', but earlier that year he took a leading role in forming the New Zealand Labour Party, was elected to the national executive and remained a member for the rest of his life. Then, like Savage and others, he entered politics through the local city councils. As the years went by, these men moved closer to the middle ground of politics, abandoning much of the ideological policy of the extreme left before they became part of the first Labour government in 1935 – and had to deal with union problems from the other side.

Thirty-two

THE MAORI VC WINNER FROM HARROW AND CAMBRIDGE

Bizarre though it may seem, William Barnard Rhodes-Moorhouse was originally disqualified from flying for the Royal Flying Corps because he had a full set of false teeth, the result of flying and motoring accidents. The part-Maori youth had been to Harrow and Cambridge but his heart was in engineering – motorcycles, cars and aeroplanes. He escaped a manslaughter charge after a man died when a horse bucked in panic as he roared along in a fast car. He and a friend built an aircraft of their own less than a decade after the Wright Brothers first flew.

When the First World War was declared Rhodes-Moorhouse joined up as a mechanic. But he was an experienced pioneering pilot and after delivery flights of aircraft over the Channel in the early months of the war, he inveigled himself an operational job with No 2 Squadron, RFC. He flew reconnaissance missions with an observer, artillery spotting and taking photographs.

Dog-fighting was still in its infancy, with aircrew pot-shotting at each other with handguns if they could get close enough, but ground fire was dangerous for the slow, low-flying aircraft of the time.

The Second Battle of Ypres started in January 1915 and German reinforcements were routed through the railway junction at Courtrai, fifty-six kilometres behind the front line. Lieutenant-Colonel Trenchard ordered No 2 Squadron to bomb the station, a hazardous undertaking from above an area seething with troops armed with machine-guns, artillery pieces and rifles.

Rhodes-Moorhouse took on the assignment. The size of the bomb – more than forty-five kilograms – meant he had to leave his observer behind, a man called Sholto Douglas, who lived to become an Air Vice Marshall in the Second World War. He knew he would have to fly his tiny, fragile BE2b aircraft in low and be exposed to heavy fire if he was to deliver the bomb accurately, especially without an observer. Before he left, he wrote a letter to his aviator wife, Linda, explaining the dangers of the mission, and another to his infant son to be opened on his twenty-first birthday.

He approached the railway station lower than 100 metres through machine-gun fire from a nearby church belfry, and rifle and shell fire from the ground. He was wounded in his left hand and right thigh, so had to let go of the joystick and lean over to release the bomb. The bomb landed on target and caused havoc in the junction below. The blast bumped the plane almost out of control.

Rhodes-Moorhouse decided to return to base, despite his wounds, and kept the aircraft low to get back over the front line and away from enemy fire as quickly as possible. The aircraft already had more than ninety bullet holes when one shot from the ground seriously wounded him in the abdomen. Indian troops in the trenches, watching the battering the aircraft got from the ground, waved and cheered as Moorhouse crossed the line. He flew on, landed the plane faultlessly but could not move from the cockpit. He died the next day after saying that it was 'a strange thing, dying, unlike anything one has ever done before – like one's first solo flight'.

On the night of the bombing, the British Commander, General Sir John French, said in his daily bulletin to the troops that it was 'the most important bomb dropped in the war so far'. Rhodes-Moorhouse was posthumously awarded the Victoria Cross, the first airman to be so honoured.

His background reads like a Gothic novel with a plot line that runs all the way back to New Zealand. His grandfather was William Barnard Rhodes, oldest of four pioneering brothers who came from Yorkshire and developed the famous Levels property at Timaru and farms in Hawke's Bay, Rangitikei and Wellington. William was a former merchant seaman and whaling-ship skipper, who established one of the first cattle stations in the South Island (at Akaroa) and trading posts in Hawke's Bay and Poverty Bay, before settling in Wellington, where he built the first wharf. He was tough, mean but very astute. Although he had substantial landholdings, his business became commerce and finance rather than farming. When he died he was one of the wealthiest men in New Zealand, leaving an estate of £4 million.

Rhodes married Sarah King, daughter of a Wellington

lawyer, who died in 1862, and then Sarah Ann Moorhouse, sister of William Sefton Moorhouse, a prominent settler who was at various times Superintendent of Canterbury, Mayor of Wellington and a Member of Parliament. Rhodes had no children by either wife but fathered an illegitimate daughter by a Maori woman called Mary, who has left no footprint in history for some unfathomable reason, no trace of a whakapapa. Maori, whom one would think would be proud to claim the grandmother of a heroic aviator, have remained silent about her identity. One claim was that she died young. Another story is that she was a 'princess', given to Rhodes by a grateful father to marry 'in the Maori way'; another that she was a family housekeeper. Some have said she was Ngai Tahu, others that she came from Te Aro.

Rhodes and his wife loved his half-Maori natural daughter, Mary Ann Rhodes, inordinately and Sarah Ann adopted her. She was intelligent and attractive and brought up with every advantage. Her father's will provided for her, but after he died she challenged it, seeking more money, first in New Zealand's Supreme Court where she lost, and then in the Privy Council, where she won and was awarded £750,000. After her father's death she married her stepmother's younger brother, Edward, in Wellington, in 1883. He was forty-nine. She was thirty-one. They moved to England and raised four children, including William Barnard Moorhouse. Shortly before he was married in 1912, William legally appended 'Rhodes' to his name in order to satisfy a demand in his grandfather's will.

Rhodes-Moorhouse was of average height but strongly built. He was described as having sandy or auburn hair and glinting green eyes, but in the official photograph held at the Henley Royal Air Force Museum, his skin colouring and the set of his eyes seem unmistakably Maori. Sarah Moorhouse and her stepdaughter told the children nothing of their Maori grandmother, perhaps because of Mary Ann's illegitimacy which may have impeded the bid for gentility their new wealth supported. Mary Ann at least once described herself as of Spanish origin.

One of William's nieces claimed that he spent some months in New Zealand in 1906–07, between leaving Harrow and starting at Cambridge, but no local evidence has been found to support this.

Rhodes-Moorhouse abandoned Cambridge and with James Radley, another pioneer aviator, built a monoplane and is said to have gone barnstorming across the United States in a Bleriot machine where, according to one claim, he became the first person to fly under the Golden Gate Bridge. He married a fellow flying enthusiast, Linda Morritt, and was the first pilot to fly the English Channel with two passengers – his wife and a *London Evening News* journalist. The flight ended with a crash-landing in bad weather in southern England and his wife suffered a miscarriage. For a few months, he abandoned flying and returned to motor racing and rallying.

Many other unofficial claims have been made for Rhodes-Moorhouse as an aviation pioneer – that he was the first to loop-the-loop, for example – and there is no doubt that he was trailblazer both as a mechanic and a pilot.

His son, also William, less than a year old when he died, went to Eton and gained a pilot's licence at age sixteen. He represented England as a skier. In 1937, with hundreds of flying hours to his credit, he joined the Royal Air Force. He took part in the first fighter-bomber attack of the Second World War in 1939, flying a Blenheim. He transferred to Hurricane fighters for the Battle of Britain, was an ace and awarded the DFC in August 1940, less than a month before he was shot down and killed over Kent. He had, no doubt, by then read his father's letter.

When Rhodes-Moorhouse died in France in 1915, the family received special dispensation to have his body returned to England for burial. He was interred in a fenced grave above the family manor, Parnham House, in Dorset, on a plateau where he and his wife had planned a house of their own. His son's body was buried alongside him on this hill. Untidy now and no longer part of the Parnham House property, this tiny cemetery is a sad reminder of the cost to a family of two world wars.

Thirty-three

DEATH IN THE DEEP GREY MUD

New Zealanders couldn't charge for death or glory across the terrain at Passchendaele in October 1917. They were trapped in deep grey mud and many of them drowned in it. Others were blown to pieces – first by their own misdirected artillery and then by the German barrage – as they struggled, waist deep, to get at the enemy. No single disaster in New Zealand history before or since could match the carnage of that one twenty-four-hour period – 640 were killed and 2100 wounded. The horror of this day was subsumed by the overall, drawn-out suffering of the war in France; and the starkness of it was shrouded by journalists, complicit with army and civil authorities in enlivening the morale myth of 'giving' your life for God, King and Country.

Field Marshal Sir Douglas Haig was a plodding, unimaginative man who commanded the British forces in France through most of the First World War. He delayed his offensive at the Third Battle of Ypres for so long with meticulous, pedantic preparation that the predictable autumn deluge swamped the area.

The Third Battle of Ypres began on July 31 and ended in November when Canadian troops finally overcame German resistance. The ridge at Passchendaele dominated what was called the Ypres Salient. As German and British artillery barrages continued over the weeks, the area was churned into great lakes of mud.

The New Zealand Division's First and Fourth Brigades achieved their targets in attacks that began on 4 October, although they suffered 1700 casualties. The reports of this first foray read like accounts of a football match. Philip Gibbs, a famous foreign correspondent, wrote that it was for Australians and New Zealanders 'their greatest and most glorious day. Fighting up Abraham Heights, they captured over 2000 prisoners. They describe the number of German dead as unprecedented . . . The New Zealanders and English admit that the German often showed pluck while he had a dog's chance, but many ran when the attackers got close . . . Although the German barrage fell upon our men before they leapt to the assault, it happened terribly for the enemy.

'Our men . . . swept over the German assault troops, annihilating them and crushing their plan of attack . . . One can only guess at what the slaughter has been. It was slaughter in which five German divisions were involved.'

Another message from London, quoted in the *New Zealand Herald*, said, bizarrely: 'A correspondent states that the New Zealanders fought magnificently. The manner in which they brought up their guns is described as worthy of a military tournament.'

An Australian and New Zealand Press Association correspondent reported that he 'saw the New Zealanders going up to the front, greatly relieved they had not been overlooked. Their greatest anxiety had been lest the "show" would be over before they were given a chance. They were in great form, having been resting since Messines, and were never keener to meet the enemy.'

Another dispatch to the *Herald* said: 'All over the battlefield there are many German dead. They can be seen in dugouts and shell holes, singly and in clusters of up to twenty. The enemy was quite demoralised by the terribly destructive fire of our barrage, which struck him in waves. The intensity of the attack and the completeness of its success, seem, at least for the time being, to have thrown his organization out of gear, even far beyond his front line.'

None of the reports mentioned the 1700 casualties.

This first foray was a matter of small news, however, compared with the disastrous second assault a week later. After the early British successes, Haig, who deployed soldiers as pawns in a game of attrition, decided to take all of the Passchendaele Ridge so he could hold a winter line there. He decided to use Australian and New Zealand troops to achieve this end.

At 5.25 a.m. on 12 October, the Second and Third Brigades of the New Zealand Army moved on to the attack. They were shelled heavily by the enemy and then mauled by misdirected friendly fire. They could move only slowly through the mud, and were further stalled by barbed-wire entanglements that had not been cut and had been booby-trapped. By the end of the day, the left flank had advanced 500 metres, the centre 200 metres and the right made no progress until late in the day when they advanced far enough to capture two blockhouses.

By the next morning when the cost was counted, the New Zealand brigades were decimated. Only two men survived from two Otago platoons. The Australian Division lost a staggering 3200 lives in the same twenty-four-hour period. It was a day that epitomises the insane futility of the First World War.

The gung-ho journalists were more muted during the later stages of the Passchendaele battle but none of them portrayed the horror with the weary accuracy of Bernard Freyberg, who fought there as a young brigade commander in the British Army. 'During the fighting, attacking companies waded knee-deep, and often up to their waists in mud before gaining their objectives, while, in many cases, whole waves disappeared, or were held captive in the mud within speaking distance of the British line, until they either died from exposure or were blown to pieces by artillery fire. It was a most wicked battle and the night after any attack, men with ladders and ropes worked away in the most appalling danger, trying to save those who were bogged.'

Freyberg was hit by shrapnel during the battle, the ninth time he had been wounded during the war.

Thirty-four

HARRY HILLS DUPES THE SEA WOLF

Inspector Harry Hills, a New Zealander with the Fijian National Constabulary, pulled off a great bluff to capture the German sea raider Count Felix von Luckner during the First World War. The Germans were lurking in a ship's boat on Wakaya, an atoll on the fringe of the Fijian group. They had rested and taken on supplies after an epic voyage across the Pacific almost as far as Captain Bligh sailed after he was dumped from HMS *Bounty*. They were preparing to leave the atoll in a bid to capture a ship to replace the one they had wrecked on the island of Mopelia, in the Society Islands.

Hills was aboard an island steamer, *Amra*. The only armament on board was his empty service revolver. He was looking for the foreign men in a small boat, suspecting they were Germans. *Amra* anchored across the narrow opening in the reef and Hills and some of his men rowed in close. He stood up in his boat, his hand on his revolver, and ordered them to surrender. The steamer, he said, had them covered.

The bluff worked. The Germans gave in even though they had concealed aboard their vessel a machine-gun, thousands of rounds of ammunition, grenades and rifles. Thus was von Luckner, the 'Sea Devil', duped, captured, taken to New Zealand and imprisoned on Motuihi Island in the Hauraki Gulf. But in the game of deception and bluff, von Luckner was also very accomplished and by the war's end he emerged as a chivalrous hero to the British, and especially to New Zealanders.

His exploits would not have been possible in the modern age of helicopters, telecommunications and satellite spying. They read like a tale of derring-do from one of the boys' magazines of the time, partly because of his panache and daring and rare wartime humanity, but also because he told his own story and on at least one occasion embroidered the narrative to his advantage.

As a thirteen-year-old, von Luckner ran away to sea, worked on vessels for a number of shipping companies mainly in the Pacific, spent time ashore at various jobs in Australia and America, and then returned home with enough money to graduate from the Lubeck Navigation School and join the German Navy. Early in the First World War, he fought in the battles of Heligoland and Jutland, was wounded at Jutland but rescued after his ship went down. Then he was chosen for an unusual mission as captain of what had been an American clipper ship, *Pass of Balmaha*.

The *Seeadler* (Sea Eagle), as it was renamed by the Germans – or the *Irma*, a Norwegian merchant ship bound for Melbourne, as it was called in the falsified papers it carried – was fitted with an auxiliary engine, and carried two concealed 105-mm guns, as well as machine-guns, bombs and small arms. It had accommodation for prisoners. Von Luckner and his sixty-four crew were to leave from Heligoland, bluff their way through the Royal Navy's blockade of German ports, sail down the Atlantic and into the Pacific, and there to disrupt the shipping services to Europe by capturing and sinking as much tonnage as they could. When boarded by a party from a Royal Navy ship, *Avenger*, crewed mostly by New Zealanders, 'A Long Way to Tipperary' was playing on a gramophone and whisky was handed around among the visitors, who left, satisfied by the bogus papers.

Von Luckner had by far his biggest success as a raider while on his way down the Atlantic to Cape Horn. The disguised sailing ship lured eleven enemy vessels into its web and sank them before he even got into the Pacific, and not one life was lost. Von Luckner said later: 'Before I gave the order to sink any of the many ships we accounted for, I took care to see even the ship's cat was safe.'

In the Pacific, he was much less successful. He sank three small American ships, again without killing anyone, but when his ship's doctor reported signs of beriberi or scurvy among the crew, he decided to stop at Mopelia, the most remote of the Society Islands, which he believed was uninhabited, for rest and resuscitation and supplies.

There the *Seeadler* was wrecked. How? Several versions have been offered, the most unlikely by von Luckner. In his accounts of the event to his biographer Lowell Thomas in *The Sea Devil*, and to others, he talked of a tidal wave ten or twelve metres high caused by an undersea earthquake that grabbed the ship, lifted it up and crashed it down on the coral reef. When the wave had passed, the proud *Seeadler* lay smashed to pieces, reduced to a wreck on the coral reef.

His story was picked up even by naval historians but it was almost certainly a fabrication. No one was killed or even badly injured. Nowhere else was a tsunami reported. What probably happened, according to accounts by other members of his crew, was that von Luckner and the other German officers, except for one left on board, went ashore for a picnic, leaving the *Seeadler* anchored to the coral with sails set to hold her off the island. The wind changed, the sea got up quickly and the vessel was dashed upon the coral, its propeller damaged beyond repair, rendering the engine useless. Von Luckner's elaborate tsunami tale was to avoid court-martials for himself and others. Because the masts were still visible, the crew attempted to break them with explosives and in the process the ship was accidentally destroyed by fire.

Von Luckner buried money and other valuables and the ship's logbook before setting out in the eighteen-foot ship's sailboat with five others in a bid to capture a larger ship, return to pick up his full complement and continue harassing British and American shipping. They called at Atiu, Aitutaki and Rarotonga in the Cook Islands, posing as Dutch-Americans on an island cruise. They rowed and sailed for 3700 kilometres without finding a vulnerable vessel, and eventually arrived at Wakaya, where Harry Hills called their bluff.

In October 1917, Von Luckner and one of his officers were interned on Motuihi in the Hauraki Gulf with other Germans, mainly prisoners of war taken during New Zealand's successful campaign in Samoa early in the war. He immediately began planning their escape. By 13 December, they had manufactured bombs in tin cans, stolen two pistols and a sword, assembled charts, including one of the Hauraki Gulf and its minefields, and fashioned a sextant. An inmate who helped maintain the thirty-five-foot, fifteen-horsepower island launch *Pearl* had established a stash of food and water aboard. That night they cut the telephone line to Auckland, set fire to the barracks to divert the guards, and twelve prisoners quietly slipped away in the launch.

By the time communications with Auckland were restored the next morning, *Pearl* was 110 kilometres away, off the east coast of Coromandel, where two days later they boarded the sailing scow *Moa* and set off for the Kermadecs, which von Luckner intended to use as a base to capture a larger vessel. But the captain of another scow, *Rangi*, had seen what happened to the *Moa*, reported the incident and soon the *Iris*, an auxiliary cruiser armed with two six-pounder guns, was in pursuit. Von Luckner was on Curtis Island in the Kermadecs when he saw the smoke from the *Iris* and attempted to flee with the *Moa* in full sail. A shell across the bow convinced the Germans to surrender.

The escapers spent fourteen days in Mt Eden prison, six months on Ripa Island in Lyttelton Harbour and then went back to Motuihi. Von Luckner twice planned escapes, including through a tunnel he started digging, but both were unsuccessful and he was repatriated after the war.

Apart perhaps from the Red Baron, he was the only German combatant in the First World War to become a hero to the other side, respected for his humanity (he claimed he never killed anyone in the war) and admired for his daring and skill. He managed this at a time when Germans had been demonised in New Zealand to the point where a German-born, English-educated, widely respected academic at Victoria University College in Wellington, Professor George von Zedlitz, was sacked from his job after twelve years there and publicly ostracised by politicians, despite the support of his fellow academics.

In Europe, von Luckner became a celebrated touring lecturer during the 1920s but then his star waned as he became a propagandist for the Nazis. When he arrived in New Zealand aboard his yacht *Seeteufel* (Sea Devil) in 1938, he was fêted at first but then many came to regard him as a Nazi propagandist and spy. His comment on that was: 'To think I would travel 1600 miles from Germany to talk politics. Why, it is ridiculous. I am but a sailor and know nothing of politics. I respect Herr Hitler, as I do the German government, but I take no part in it. If I am an ambassador, let me be one of peace.' But the legend was fading by the time of his visit as the Nazis shaped Germany up for another war.

Footnote: The castaways left on Mopelia captured a small ship that put in there and attempted to sail home, but the vessel was wrecked near Easter Island and they spent the rest of the war imprisoned in Chile. While he was in the Pacific in 1938, von Luckner called at Mopelia and dug up the money and papers he had buried there more than twenty years before.

Thirty-five

DEATH COMES WITH THE PRIME MINISTER

When the SS *Niagara* pulled into the wharf at Auckland on 12 October 1918, Prime Minister William Massey and Minister of Finance Sir Joseph Ward were aboard, along with a lethal supernumerary – the pneumonic influenza virus. The fact the ship was allowed to berth and was not quarantined became a scandal. A radio message as she approached the coast sought urgent hospital accommodation for twenty-five people seriously ill with the Spanish flu – among the 100 who had gone down with it.

By the time the ship pulled alongside, 130 people had contracted the disease, and the boatswain, Thomas Rutherford, had died from it. The government had known of the influenza pandemic that was racing around the world in the dying months of the First World War, and many New Zealanders decided the ship was not quarantined because Massey and Ward wanted to get off it. Massey's Reform Party held power and Ward, leader of the Liberal Party, was part of the special wartime Cabinet. They didn't like each other much but had travelled together to a conference in London. When the accusation was made in Parliament that the ship had avoided quarantine only because of their presence, Ward abhorred what he termed a 'wicked statement'.

What was certain was that the epidemic arrived about the same time as the *Niagara* and spread out from Auckland. During the six months until autumn the following year when the disease pretty well ran its course, more than 6700 died in New Zealand, including an estimated 1200 Maori (a figure since challenged as a very rough guess and serious underestimate). Deaths around the world were estimated at twenty-one million. In terms of both global reach and the total death toll, it was history's worst pandemic.

One reason public-health authorities were lax in allowing the ship in was that New Zealand had no experience of epidemics of the virulence of that influenza. Polynesians had outrun the pandemic diseases, such as malaria, as they sped out into the Pacific centuries before, and Maori had inherited this protection afforded by distance. But, because they had built up no immunity, all Polynesians suffered high mortality rates from relatively mild imported diseases like measles in the early days of their connection to European visitors. More severe were the consequences of tuberculosis and venereal diseases.

A few years before, from about 1910, smallpox had spread at abnormal levels, and outbreaks of diphtheria occurred occasionally. From 1920 onwards, poliomyelitis (or 'infantile paralysis', as it was popularly called) spread dangerously, usually during the hottest summer months, and caused school closures to prevent contagion – the last time in 1947, not long before the Salk vaccine became available.

But because of New Zealand's distance from the world's main centres of population and the high standard of diet and public health, epidemics of diseases like the bubonic plague that had scythed through Europe for hundreds of years were unknown here. (One bubonic case occurred in the opening years of the twentieth century.) This was the country's first plague and remains easily the most devastating. Victims began by shivering wildly, no matter the temperature of their environment. Headaches, sneezing and coughing usually followed, accompanied by extreme physical weariness and mental depression. Many people recovered but took a long time to overcome extreme lethargy and regain full health.

The disease had its worst effect in the high-population areas because denser population helped its contagion. Local-body meetings were postponed, theatres, cinemas and pubs closed, sporting events called off and even some churches closed and advised parishioners to attend to their devotions at home. Some people left the cities, just as the aristocracy had fled London at the first signs of one of the regular plagues that hit England over the centuries.

Sixteen hundred and eighty people died of the flu in Auckland and 1406 in Wellington. Although the death toll was lower in the provincial areas, the disease seemed to gain power as it moved south, with a particularly virulent strain in Christchurch.

The deaths cut deeply into public morale. About 18,000 New Zealanders had died and 50,000 were wounded on active service during the four years of the

First World War, which ended exactly one month after the flu arrived. During that month, the names of the epidemic victims were published in newspapers alongside the final casualty lists from the war.

In Auckland, the impact on public services was immediate and severe. Before the end of October, seventeen out of twenty firemen in Auckland City were ill, twelve of the sixty-five police were stricken, and sickness rates among staff meant suburban train services were suspended and bus services reduced. Fifty Auckland Public Hospital nurses caught the virus. Victoria Park in Auckland was used as a morgue until the health authorities ruled that all those who died of the flu or its complications were to be buried as soon as possible on the strength of a doctor's certificate, without any inquests.

Dr Doris Gordon, a legendary general practitioner, was working in Stratford at the time. She contracted the flu and wrote in the brisk, no-nonsense style that made her later autobiographical books nationally popular: 'While I was still abed, the joy bells for the truce with Germany rang out. For years I'd lived and prayed for this moment and now it found me pickled in toxins, aspirins and quinine. In the next bedroom was my sister-in-law equally ill . . . I staggered into her room and pitched myself on the foot of her bed – I had just enough humour left to think what a queer pair of jubilant soldiers' wives we looked – and croaked, "Dot, that's peace and they are not killed yet!"

'Unfortunately many moderately infected cases got out of bed on that Armistice Day; for youth in full flush of adolescent enthusiasm could not remain in bed for an ache and cough when Stratford's Broadway was *en fête*.

As a result many mild cases developed complications and as the disease leapt from case to case it enhanced its virulence until many people were stricken from the outset with lethal infection which turned them first dusky blue and then petechial purple.

'When I resumed work, finding even the doctor's bag a trial to carry, I had the whole district on my hands, a more virulent type of disease, civil panic and total disorganisation of services . . . Funeral processions were banned and often relatives had to help the over-worked gravediggers.'

Dr Gordon's anecdotal evidence confirmed what was later deduced from official records – that males were infected at about twice the rate of females and, once infected, had less chance of recovery.

Did the *Niagara* bring the disease into Auckland, and would it have been quarantined if Massey and Ward had not been on board? First of all, influenza was not officially a notifiable disease and the Minister of Health would have had to take special action to keep the ship out, although many historians accept that had Massey and Ward not been aboard he probably would have done so. The *New Zealand Herald* had reported a growing number of flu cases in Auckland during early October, before the ship arrived, but no deaths. Outbreaks of the disease in army camps at Auckland, Featherston and Trentham, in Wellington, had also been reported and several deaths had occurred in Napier. It was almost certainly here or would have arrived anyway, but probably not with the dramatic swiftness and intensity that occurred after the *Niagara* arrived with its concentrated infection.

A Commission of Inquiry headed by Mr Justice

Denniston was firm in its finding that 'although the matter is not one capable of absolute demonstration, the evidence before us provides a very special presumption that a substantial factor in the introduction of the epidemic was the arrival in Auckland on October 12 of the SS *Niagara* with patients infected with the epidemic disease.'

The commission also noted an even more disastrous consequence of failure to quarantine. The SS *Talune*, berthed alongside the *Niagara*, soon had crew infected and yet was allowed to sail to Apia and dock there, with devastating effects among Samoans. By the end of the year, before the epidemic waned, 7500 of 38,000 Samoans had died of the disease.

Footnote: The 13,415-tonne SS *Niagara* ended its life spectacularly twenty-two years later when it struck a German mine only forty-five kilometres off the Whangarei Heads at three o'clock in the morning of 19 June 1940. Several German raiders were present in the Tasman Sea and South Pacific in the early years of the war. Their attacks on cargo ships and the mines they laid sank not only the *Niagara* but the 16,712-tonne *Rangitane*, a small steamer, the *Holmwood*, the even smaller *Puriri* and five other small vessels further north in the Pacific. These losses caused concern among the authorities in Australia and New Zealand but the public was told nothing at the time.

The *Niagara's* complement of 349 took to the boats, and the rescue operation in response to the radio alert as she sank was so swiftly successful they were all back in Auckland by that night. But what they didn't have with them was gold bullion worth more than two and a half million pounds sterling, owned by the Bank of England and on its way to the United States. War or no war, search and recovery operations started immediately. By the end of 1941, a Melbourne firm had located the wreck and in an epic act of salvage retrieved all but about £150,000 worth. As the price of gold went up, other salvagers recovered more of the bullion.

Thirty-six

THE DISDAIN OF A COW'S RAISED TAIL

When Ernest Rutherford died, a Nobel Prize-winning contemporary, Max Born, called him the greatest scientist he had ever known, and that included Einstein. And yet if you ask most New Zealanders who he was they will recite, almost chant, the phrase, 'He was the first man to split the atom.'

Rutherford is almost forgotten beyond that phrase, which seems to suggest he achieved just one thing in isolation from an otherwise uneventful career, through some stroke of scientific luck. In a great moment of New Zealand and world history, in 1919 he achieved the dream of the ages, alchemy, by turning nitrogen into hydrogen and oxygen. That was the peak but it was one event among many notable achievements.

The English scientist Sir Robert Robinson, a contemporary of Rutherford's, wrote in the middle of the twentieth century that 'he was the father of nuclear physics. The inspired interpretation of his observations and his genius for experiment led to practically all we know about the structure of the atom . . . He always worked on problems at the limits of human knowledge.' He was, Robinson insisted, 'the greatest physical scientist of his age'.

Rutherford won the Nobel Prize for chemistry at thirty-six and, according to his biographer, New Zealand physicist John Campbell, he 'altered our view of nature on three occasions': first, when he 'explained the perplexing problem of naturally occurring radioactivity'; second, when he described the structure of an atom; and third, when he artificially altered that structure.

After that, in 1932, working with John Cockroft and Ernest Walton, he developed a new type of machine, a proton accelerator, which further advanced artificial transmutation by using particles of hydrogen, accelerated to enormous speeds, as projectiles. He was for forty years involved in many innovative and important experiments of discovery – from the time he became a research student at Cambridge's Cavendish Laboratory, until he was its director. Cavendish was the finest physics laboratory in the British Empire at the time and one of the most notable in the world. Rutherford was knighted in 1914, admitted to the exclusive Order of Merit in 1925, and became Baron Rutherford of Nelson in 1932. And yet, despite his widespread fame, and although just about every New Zealander had heard of him, few people even today know anything much about him and his work beyond the rote line that he 'split the atom'.

For twenty years, Campbell made it his task to restore the nation's consciousness of Rutherford's achievements. He decided 'to remedy a nation's neglect' of a man he considered its greatest son. He wrote: 'In 1987, on the 50th anniversary of the death of Ernest Rutherford, the state of the place of his birth remained a national disgrace. I went there at dawn and gazed despairingly at the untidy piles of the river boulders, which had been dumped on the site many years previously. In the field beyond, a cow raised its tail and spoke for me.'

The neglect was pervasive, and the ignorance bordered on the contemptuous. Even a Prime Minister indulged the common mistake that Rutherford was awarded the Nobel Prize for splitting the atom. Campbell noted that a plaque at Canterbury University College incorrectly recorded the date of his enrolment, and for many years 'one of New Zealand's foremost public companies, which built Rutherford House as its head office, worshipped a portrait of the curator of the Otago Museum, mistakenly believing it to be Lord Rutherford's'. Campbell became convenor of the Rutherford Birthplace Project and was largely responsible for the memorial that has graced this site at Brightwater, Nelson, since the 1990s. Milestones from his life and work are annotated in a beautifully laid out garden.

Rutherford was born in 1871, the fourth of twelve children. His father farmed and processed flax. Later, after Ernest had gone to Nelson College, the family moved to Taranaki. He was christened 'Earnest', probably in error but, at the time of his marriage, decided on the importance of being Ernest and henceforth dropped the 'a'. He was known among family, friends and colleagues as 'Ern'. He went to local primary schools and won a scholarship, at the second attempt, to Nelson College where he was head boy and dux in 1889. Rutherford said later that had he not won that scholarship at his second attempt, he would probably have become a farmer.

At Nelson, he sat the Junior National Scholarship, was fourth on the scholarship list with passes in Latin, English, French, mathematics, sound and light, and mechanics. From there he won, again at the second attempt, a scholarship to Canterbury University College. But for all this, he was not as brilliant at primary or secondary school as some embellished accounts insist, according to Campbell. His contemporaries at Foxhill and Havelock Primary Schools were surprised he did well, and did not remember him except as a quiet kid and something of a swot. His professors at Canterbury College mostly considered him less promising than two of his contemporaries.

Rutherford was a tall, robust man, later famous for a stentorian voice. He played rugby as a forward and took a full part in university life. He certainly developed intellectually there, taking an MA with double first-class honours in mathematics and mathematical physics and in physical science (electricity and magnetism). That was in 1893. The following year he gained a BSc in geology and chemistry.

His first career choice was to be a teacher but he failed to get a permanent job so tried for a scholarship to Cambridge University. He came second, but was able to take it up when the winner, Auckland scholar James McLaurin, turned it down. By the time Rutherford left New Zealand in 1895, he had established a local reputation as an innovative researcher working in the area of electrical science. At Cambridge, he became the first student who was not a Cambridge graduate to work under Professor JJ Thomson at the Cavendish. It was an opportune time to be there as Thomson was setting out in new research directions.

At twenty-seven Rutherford was appointed to the chair of physics at Montreal's McGill University, which had an internationally respected physics laboratory. Over the following eight years his work in the area of atomic research was trail-blazing and his results at McGill won him the Nobel Prize for Chemistry. In 1907 he became Professor of Physics at the University of Manchester and the following year he won the Bressa Prize from the Turin Academy of Science, which declared that his work over the previous three years had, in its opinion, been the most important and distinguished of any research in any branch of science.

His first seminal discovery was of the nuclear structure of the atom, which was later described as the peak of his achievement and one that would remain a prominent landmark in the history of science. But more was to come. After an interruption to do scientific work for the Royal Navy during the First World War, having hypothesised on the structure of the atom, he set about experiments that would change that structure by breaking up an atom. He thus became the world's first alchemist, bombarding nitrogen atoms with alpha particles and, by altering its atomic structure, turning nitrogen into hydrogen and oxygen.

Rutherford died suddenly in October 1937 from complications after a hernia operation. He was sixty-six. Tributes poured in from around the world, and his ashes were deposited in Westminster Abbey near the tombs of Isaac Newton and Charles Darwin. He was remembered not only as a great scientist but at a personal level for his striking personality and his generosity. Lord Baldwin said of him: 'His refreshing personality, his dauntless spirit, the merry twinkle of his eye, the exuberance of his ever-youthful, ever-joyful enthusiasm; how can they be recaptured; one can only say he was a peer among men'. An Australian colleague, WH Bragg, wrote: 'Rutherford has upset many theories but he has never belittled anyone's work . . . He takes always the broad and generous view, readily giving credit to others for their contributions to knowledge and never pressing for the recognition of his own.'

Over the years he encouraged many young New Zealand science students to study in Britain and arranged for some of them to work with him. When he became Lord Rutherford he designed a coat of arms that included a kiwi and a Maori warrior. He returned to New Zealand for four visits, the first in 1900 to marry Mary Newton, the daughter of his Christchurch landlady; the second in 1905; the third in 1914; and the last in 1925 when he toured Australia and New Zealand, lecturing in the main centres and to students, including those at his old school in Nelson.

After his death, Rutherford's name was readily remembered in his homeland but the magnitude of his achievement was largely forgotten, and remains insufficiently understood.

Thirty–seven

A MAN GOOD AT SUMS, AND ONE
WHO READ THE BIBLE IN SWAHILI

Alex Aitken from Dunedin never really knew whether it was his astonishing memory or some unrecognised facility of mind that enabled him to multiply 987,654,321 by 123,456,789 in his head and come up with the correct answer in thirty seconds; or to convert four forty-sevenths into decimals to twenty-six places in four seconds. He suspected it was a combination of both. A psychologist at Edinburgh University where Professor Aitken taught for many years from the mid-1920s probed his mind and said that numbers seemed to play a tune in the great mathematician's mind, 'like a Bach fugue'.

Twenty years older than Aitken, Harold Williams, from Auckland, joined *The Times* of London in 1921 as foreign editor, which enabled the newspaper to take advantage of his fluency in fifty-eight languages. A great supporter of the League of Nations, he was the only person attending meetings of the league in Geneva who could talk to every delegate in his own language.

Although extraordinary, these are only two of the hundreds of people who, since the nineteenth century, have confirmed a fact of New Zealand history – that the country loses its greatest talents to larger countries because New Zealand is not a big enough stage for them. This gift of talented people has been astonishingly rich and diverse. The reverse migration began before the end of the nineteenth century and it continues.

In the mid-1970s, novelist and essayist VS Naipaul, in *The Return of Eva Peron*, a book-length commentary on Argentina, wrote it 'has diminished and stultified the men whom it attracted by the promise of ease and to whom it offered no other ideals and no new idea of human association. New Zealand, equally colonial, also with a past of native dispossession, but founded at an earlier imperial period and on different principles, has had a different history. It has made some contribution to the world; more gifted men and women have come from its population of three million than from the twenty-three millions of Argentines . . .'

If this comparison is odious to Argentina, it is by no means over-flattering to New Zealand. The 1966 *Encyclopaedia of New Zealand* listed thousands of living expatriates who had achieved eminence in dozens of countries, including hundreds in Britain or the British Colonial Service. Even Argentina benefited. AA Cameron of Hakataramea became a legendary figure there and in Chile after moving there in 1893 and establishing the largest sheep station in the world in Tierra del Fuego.

Examples of this excellence include the plastic surgeon Archibald McIndoe who became the best-known plastic surgeon of his time, and a great humanist. After graduating from Dunedin Medical School in 1923, he earned an MSc from the University of Minnesota in 1927 and then worked under Sir Harold Gillies – also a New Zealander and a cousin of McIndoe's – in the new specialty of plastic surgery at St Bartholomew's Hospital in London. He earned fame and the gratitude of hundreds of airmen during and after the Second World War at the Queen Victoria Hospital where he helped surgically and psychologically to repair serious damage from burns incurred by air crew. His 'Guinea-pig Club' brought him lasting respect among airmen and from his professional peers. He also had great personal warmth and charm, and was an accomplished pianist – no surprise, perhaps, to those who knew his mother was a fine singer and sister of the pre-eminent New Zealand composer and musician of his time, Alfred Hill.

McIndoe's much-publicised feats in the Second World War have tended to obscure the fact that Harold Gillies was a similar figure during the First World War, perhaps even more of a trail-blazer in their chosen profession. Like McIndoe, Gillies was born in Dunedin. He was educated at Wanganui Collegiate, where he captained the first eleven and represented Wanganui at cricket, including in a match against Australia. He went to Cambridge, rowed against Oxford, and represented his university at golf for three years. He specialised first in ear, nose and throat medicine and became interested in plastic surgery in 1914 when, as a member of the Royal Army Medical Corps, he watched a French surgeon at work. From then on, during and after the war, Gillies devoted his time to remodelling damaged or malformed faces. His became so famous that when King Leopold of Belgium was injured in a car accident, Gillies was consulted and gave him virtually a new face. If McIndoe was the famous, accomplished son of plastic surgery, Gillies was the father of the specialty in Britain. An extraordinarily versatile man, he represented England at golf, was a good enough painter to have highly publicised exhibitions in London, and travelled widely in Europe to indulge his passion for fly-fishing.

Professor Alexander Aitken was born in Dunedin in 1895 and became dux of Otago Boys' High School, but university studies were interrupted by the First World War. He first began to understand the amazing nature of his memory as an infantryman on Gallipoli by memorising numerical details of his fellow soldiers, down to the serial numbers of their rifles. Wounded in France, he was sent home and graduated from Otago University in 1919 with first-class honours in Latin and French and second-class honours in mathematics. He gained a postgraduate scholarship to Edinburgh University, where he graduated as a doctor of science.

After a stage demonstration of his intuitive arithmetic to other mathematicians at Southampton when he was still in his twenties, he was asked how he did it. He said he divided the figures into sets of five and submitted them to the rhythm of a German waltz tune. Aitken was constantly, almost reflexively imposing problems on his mind. He once said: 'If I see a motor car with the registration number 731, I can't help observing that it is seventeen times forty-three. Sometimes I find myself squaring the numbers on the lapels of bus conductors.'

Apart from the famous cabaret-act style of his mental

arithmetic, Aitken became a widely admired mathematician with extensive original work, which earned him many awards and honorary doctorates. He was Professor of Mathematics at Edinburgh from 1946 and became only the fourth New Zealander elected to a fellowship of the Royal Society. He also wrote a war memoir, *Gallipoli to the Somme*, which had an introduction by Sir Bernard Fergusson, a Governor-General of New Zealand. Aitken died in Edinburgh in 1967.

Harold Williams was born in Auckland in 1876. His father was president of the Australasian Wesleyan Methodist Church and editor of the *Methodist Times*. Williams taught himself Latin, Greek, Hebrew and most of the European languages as a boy. He entered the Methodist Ministry but then sailed for Germany in 1900 and spent three years at the University of Munich. He joined the staff of *The Times* at Stuttgart where he met and married Ariadna Tyrkova, the first woman to be elected to the Russian Duma. In 1905, he went to Russia and worked there for fourteen years writing for *The Times*, the *Manchester Guardian*, London's *Daily Chronicle* and American newspapers. He returned to London in 1918 and rejoined *The Times* in 1921.

Williams read the Bible in twenty-six languages, including Hausa, Zulu and Swahili. His light reading consisted of grammars. He was a brilliant analytical journalist but a gentle unassuming man of whom *The Times* said in its obituary, when he died at only fifty-two, that his only fault was modesty. Perhaps it was because of his shyness that he remains New Zealand's most neglected genius, the greatest linguist of his time.

Footnote: According to Eugene Grayland in *Famous New Zealanders*, the answer Professor Aitken gave to problem one was 121,932,631,112,635,269; and to problem two, decimal point 0851063829787234 0425531914.

Thirty-eight

THE POWER OF PRAYER VERSUS
THE PULL OF THE PINT

A skein of eighty soberly dressed women wound along the street from the Baptist Church at Otahuhu to the newly completed Waitemata Brewery. As members of the Women's Christian Temperance Union, they bore anti-liquor banners and the moral burden of the Puritan tradition. The 'temperance' in their organisation's name was something of a euphemism, for national prohibition was their true aim.

Assembled on the lawn outside the brewery – with 'heads held high, shining eyes and . . . strong resolution', as one newspaper put it – they urged God and man through prayer and placards to divert the building from its purpose-built role into a factory for food or clothing. But neither God nor man was taking notice as the women, each flaunting the blue ribbon of the WCTU, made their speeches, proclaimed their prayers and sang their hymns. 'It was a remarkable march and demonstration without precedent in Auckland,' reported the *Auckland*

Star. A crowd of spectators joined the throng outside the building while inside the brewery management and invited guests scornfully toasted the success of the new brand of beer.

The prohibition movement's command centre, the Alliance, had lobbied the government to withdraw the new brewery licence but all they received was an assurance that no more would be issued. So the movement's shock troops, the members of the WCTU, moved into action. They held protest meetings around the country and then launched the final assault on the day the brewery opened. To no avail.

The year was 1929. The country was skidding into economic depression but prospects for brewers looked better than they had for half a century. The near-monopoly of New Zealand Breweries was turning a better profit year by year, and in the 1928 triennial liquor poll, support for the prohibition movement showed signs of falling away rapidly from its peak in 1919. So Dominion Breweries was born and, as no more brewing licences were issued for more than twenty years, it flourished, after a shaky start. The duopoly of NZB and DB ensured a high-volume, low-choice drinking culture inside scungy hotels for decades to come.

The prohibitionists' power was far from expended, though. For another thirty years they still had enough electoral muscle to intimidate governments into making no move towards liberalisation of licensing laws. Because of possible electoral consequences, governments from the nineteenth century deflected responsibility for change by holding regular referendums on who would produce alcoholic beverages, who would sell them and where and when they could be sold. When pressure from the Alliance or the brewers became too great, Commissions of Inquiry into the liquor industry were held to stall action and ensure minimum movement. A committee of the Legislative Council was the first, in 1902, and thereafter committees or commissions into liquor regulation were held in 1922, 1945, 1960 and 1974. Recommendations were attended to or ignored according to the politics of the day but no real changes were made until 1960, and for some years after that they were incremental.

The adage that the best way to change a bad law is to enforce it never held up when it came to New Zealand's licensing laws. For decades, men drank in hotel bars after hours and were often enough caught and fined, as were the publicans involved, despite elaborate arrangements to thwart the police who, however, were often enough complicit in allowing the illegal drinking to go on.

Similar ruses were increasingly employed by restaurateurs and cabaret operators to provide diners, surreptitiously, with wine to accompany their meals. For generations, only hotel restaurants had had the privilege of serving liquor with meals, a monopoly they had enjoyed without much style or enthusiasm because the real money was in serving liquor at speed in bars, not food. But pressure to liberalise licensing was coming from foreign immigrants, especially the Dutch, many of whom were in the hospitality business, and from the rapidly increasing number of New Zealanders returning from visits to other countries as the age of jet travel began.

As a result, in 1961, the Licensing Control Commission issued liquor licences to nine restaurants – four in Auckland, three in Wellington, one in Rotorua and one in Christchurch. Customers were allowed to order wine for consumption only at their tables and only between noon and 2.30 p.m. and between 6 p.m. and 11.30 p.m. The old puritan assumption remained – that liquor caused sexual and other behavioural lapses even among otherwise decent people. The licences were issued only to expensive restaurants with a limited number of tables, printed menus, carpeted floors, uniformed staff and other high operational standards.

But the new provisions that only the well-off could enjoy wine with their meals on a night out at a city restaurant would have been anathema to New Zealanders had such rules been imposed on any other area of social activity. As it was, some leaders did complain at the inequity of it, but it was another decade before licences began to spread out to cafés.

The moral dilemma over liquor began in 1835 in Hokianga when the honorary Additional British Resident, Thomas McDonnell, banned alcohol from the then bustling seaport and shipbuilding centre of Horeke. He had arriving ships searched and any grog found poured overboard. One of the earliest breweries in New Zealand was set up in Nelson in 1841 and the first temperance society the following year. From then for more than a hundred years, the conflict between drinkers and wowsers became central to the history of the country. In 1974, Mr JF Jeffries (later Mr Justice Jeffries) told a Royal Commission on the sale of liquor: 'the history of our liquor laws more than anything else represents a microcosm of New Zealand social history as a whole'.

Drunkenness was rife in pioneering New Zealand. In

1847, one in every eight Aucklanders was convicted for drunkenness; thirty years later, convictions throughout New Zealand reached seventeen per 1000 people. It came down from then on but abuse was still serious enough for prohibition groups to pressure the government to pass the 1881 Licensing Act, which prevented the issue of further licences for liquor sale without the specific consent provided by a poll among local ratepayers.

The most readily available, and therefore the preferred, drink of the earliest years was whisky, or some other often dangerously strong spirit; but, as the years went by, beer became the favoured drink, especially of the working class, in the warm climates of New Zealand and Australia, and that is probably why drunkenness rates gradually fell.

In 1886, the local prohibitionists got themselves nationally organised with the formation of the New Zealand Alliance for the Suppression of the Liquor Traffic. From then until the late 1960s, governments were under constant attack from the Alliance on one flank and brewing interests and drinkers on the other. A Justice Department report in the 1970s said the prohibitionist campaign 'took on the fervour of a moral crusade. They drew support from a very wide spectrum of opinion . . . In the space of a few years the temperance and prohibition campaign developed into the greatest populist movement this country has seen.'

In 1893, the 'local option' was introduced in the Alcoholic Liquor Sale Control Act, which gave local licensing districts the option to discontinue liquor sales where the 'dry' vote in the triennial poll passed sixty per cent. As a result, a number of towns and suburbs went dry over the years and by 1910 the number of licences nationally had dropped from 1719 to 1257.

Women, the principal victims of drunkenness, were at the forefront of the movement both locally and nationally through the WCTU, and they gained support in their campaign for women's suffrage from male prohibitionists. As we saw in Chapter 24, both groups were confident that, given the vote, women would help bring in national prohibition. They were nearly right. They won by a 33,000 majority in 1908 but a three-fifths majority was needed. Three years later, they again narrowly fell short of the three-fifths. Then they achieved the right to a simple majority and in 1919 won 246,104 votes to 232,208 – only to be thwarted by the votes from soldiers still serving overseas who switched the result to 264,189 against prohibition and 253,827 in favour. The result was never that close again. Ten years later the prohibition vote was down to forty per cent and by 1935 below thirty per cent.

The war between the zealous anti-alcohol warriors and drinkers was uneven. The Alliance was highly organised, with experienced, capable and overweeningly righteous community leaders and national politicians in their ranks, including Sir Robert Stout, one-time Premier and later Chief Justice. On the other side, brewers had plenty of money with which they freely bought allegiance, but drinkers had no organisation and in a puritanical society certainly no sense of moral rectitude. But an academic came to their aid, intellectually anyway.

He seemed a most unlikely champion. Dr William Salmond was an ordained Presbyterian minister and doctor of divinity, but also Professor of Mental and Moral

Philosophy at the University of Otago. He confronted the prohibitionists in 1911 with a sixty-eight-page book called *Prohibition: A Blunder*, which bore on its cover a quote from Oliver Cromwell: 'It will be an unjust and unwise jealousy to deprive a man of his natural liberty upon a supposition he may abuse it.' Inside, he made the rational case that alcohol was not in itself socially destructive but only the misuse of it. He claimed the issue was one of individual responsibility: 'A movement has passed into fanaticism when its advocates begin to claim for it an exclusive place in the counsels and in the favour of the Almighty . . . Legislation has a place, although a subordinate one, in the moral progress of the world; but severe, restrictive legislation, converting into crimes and penalising innocent acts, has no place at all.'

The Alliance published a ninety-six-page book with a point-by-point rebuttal, *Prohibition: An Effective Social Reform*, written by the national president, Dunedin solicitor AS Adams. His argument was that 'the state has a paramount duty to protect itself and its citizens even from the consequence of human sin and folly'. He insisted 'everybody knows that many of the ablest and most capable men are among the victims of the drink habit'. The real pressure of the drink evil fell most heavily on the wives and children of drinkers, not on the drinkers themselves, he said.

Salmond mentioned that Jesus Christ drank wine. Adams simply denied that the Saviour used alcoholic liquor: 'There can be no reasonable doubt that much of the wine of Palestine and, indeed, much of the wine in use in all countries of the world up to a date centuries after Christ, was not fermented.' Salmond had tried to be reasonable but he faced a fiery, emotional opponent.

Six o'clock closing of hotels became law in 1917, voted by Parliament as a wartime measure. This measure became unassailable for exactly fifty years, despite the disgusting culture of what came to be known as the six o'clock swill. The system continued because of an unholy, unspoken alliance between the prohibitionists on the one hand and brewers and hoteliers on the other. Prohibitionists thought the swill at least stopped drinkers from staying in the pub and not going home. Brewers and hoteliers knew they could pour maximum volumes of a few brands at minimum cost in the bleakly bibulous hour between the time workers finished for the day at five o'clock and the call of 'Time gentlemen, please' at six. In 1947, when a referendum was held on extending the hours to 10 p.m., the Alliance fought against it and their opponents did nothing to support an extension. The result was a majority in favour of continuing with six o'clock closing – not astonishing, perhaps, in light of the complicity of brewers and hoteliers in wanting no change.

Twenty years passed before another referendum extended the opening hours to 10 p.m. From then on the power of the Alliance sharply declined and the requirements for licences to manufacture and sell have slackened to almost nothing.

Although the Puritanism that stoked the prohibition movement in New Zealand was especially intense and the war with brewers and drinkers passionate and sometimes nasty, similar crusades were being fought in other countries. In Britain, drunkenness had become a problem since workers were herded into city tenements as a result of the Industrial Revolution. The fight was fought in Australia too.

And in 1919, the year in which prohibitionists failed by a whisker to win here, the Constitution of the United States was changed and the disastrous thirteen years of Prohibition began, bringing with it bootlegging and all its associated gangsterism.

Thirty-nine

THE FIRST CELEBRITY

George Bernard Shaw was the most internationally famous man ever to visit New Zealand when he arrived on an official tour in April 1934. The country was edging its way out of the twentieth century's worst economic depression. The visit was, in its time, a major event, and New Zealanders hung on his every word, wanting desperately to be admired. They were admired – and mercilessly patronised.

New Zealanders were proud of their social organisation and their egalitarianism, but embarrassingly sensitive about their remoteness, which imposed cultural cringe, a deep inferiority at being so distant from the intellectual and literary centres of Europe.

The impact of Shaw's continuing flow of comments on New Zealanders is hard to imagine now in a more adult, sceptical, perhaps querulous, time. In Christchurch, at the only official civic reception held for him while he was in the country, he was fawned over. The Deputy Mayor said participation in the reception gave him greater personal satisfaction than any other event previously in his public career; and Professor James Shelley said that Christchurch was the intellectual centre of the world by the simple fact that it contained Mr Shaw.

From the moment he arrived in Auckland on the *Rangitane*, Shaw demonstrated he knew how to exploit the new media of radio and film newsreels. It was a preamble to the age of the electronic celebrity. The *Auckland Star* reported his arrival: 'It was a typical Shavian scene which a privileged few witnessed on the deck, where in brilliant sunshine Mr Shaw made his appearance. With mock solemnity he rehearsed the incident of walking up to the camera. Head down and hands behind back, he walked slowly along, and then looking up smartly and smiling broadly, said: "Oh, good morning ladies and gentlemen. I suppose you have seen at least fifty million pictures of me. You want to see the animal walk about and you want to hear the animal talk".'

As he spoke to reporters and at public gatherings, Shaw lauded Soviet Russia; said New Zealand was really a communist country but professed to despise communism; said parliamentary democracy was obstructive and would soon be obsolete; advocated the nationalisation of land and industry; denounced tourism as an unsatisfactory industry; and proclaimed that 'what the world needed and was getting under dictators was rigid discipline'.

And if the newspaper reports are accurate, he was challenged only twice at public meetings – once by Peter Fraser when he claimed that all Labour MPs became conservatives once elected, and once by a heckler.

Shaw was the most successful playwright of his time, especially quick-witted, a leading music critic, a radical thinker and garrulous social commentator, but his greatest genius was for self-promotion. He was a tall, stringy, red-haired, vegetarian teetotaller who was seventy-eight when he visited. He made a point of prancing around like a younger man as though to demonstrate his victory over age. During a public address at the Chateau, he declared that he was 'such an extremely important person' because 'my business in life has been to stir up people's ideas and hold up their ideas and say, "Do you really believe them?"'

He urged New Zealand to stop making just butter and produce something else.

'What?' asked a member of his audience.

'Start producing brains, perhaps,' he replied.

Shaw and his wife toured the country for a month with a car and chauffeur provided by the Tourist Department, which also managed his itinerary. He drew crowds that only a pop superstar could manage today and was asked deferential questions by citizens from all walks of life.

Before him, famous visitors had been people like minor members of the Royal Family, Sidney and Beatrice Webb (celebrity socialists who came to look over the social welfare work of the Seddon government), and Lord Kitchener who came to inspect our defence forces. Writers Rudyard Kipling (who enjoyed roast kiwi in Hawke's Bay), Mark Twain and Anthony Trollope had breezed through and later wrote about this country, without any particular acuteness, as one they visited on extended tours. The only person who received a larger welcome than Shaw until commercial airlines began bringing celebrities in by the dozen in the 1970s was Queen Elizabeth II in 1953.

Two days before Shaw departed, again on the *Rangitane*, he broadcast on the only national network at the time, which was linked with Australia for the occasion. He advocated that free milk be distributed to children and added: 'I would then suggest that you go on from free milk to free bread. If you have free bread and anyone can go to a shop and get it, such a thing as a hungry child will be impossible in New Zealand.'

A broadcaster present in the studio said that immediately after the talk, the staff present began to applaud. Shaw held up his hand and said: 'Too late, we're off the air.'

When he was asked by a photographer to smile brightly for a departing photograph, he said: 'If I showed my true feelings I would cry; it's the best country I've been in.'

One extraordinary piece of cringing appeared in Rangiora's *North Canterbury Gazette* as an editorial a few days before Shaw left: 'That he regards us generally as interesting half-grown-ups who are suffering from arrested development of individuality is precisely what all visitors of distinguished intellect . . . have said about us.' The writer then offered a diagnosis of why New Zealanders were 'half-grown-up'.

A thirty-four-page booklet of his newspaper and radio coverage, entitled *What I Said in NZ: The Newspaper Utterances of Mr George Bernard Shaw*, was published soon after he left. The cover carried a picture of him holding his head in his hands. It even contained newspaper briefs on when and where he went to the theatre or to the movies. At the back it had an article called 'What GBS Eats', which listed the dietary instructions sent to hotels in advance of his arrival. Booklet price, one shilling.

Forty

EPIC JOURNEY BY OUR LITTLE
NEW ZEALAND LAMB

By the time Jean Batten arrived in Auckland from England on 16 October 1936 in her Percival Gull single-engine monoplane, the incontrovertible fact was that she was an ambitious, tough-minded and obsessive woman and possibly the most gifted aviator and navigator of her time. She had been advised against crossing the Tasman Sea – the last and most dangerous leg of what was the first direct flight from England to New Zealand – but she set off anyway, without radio or life-saving equipment. She arrived at Mangere after a flight of such precision she created a new record for the crossing: ten hours, twenty-nine minutes.

But even after that extraordinary feat, she remained locked in that female stereotype compartment men at that time could not shake from their minds. Among the 6000 people awaiting her arrival at Mangere were the Mayor of Auckland, Ernest Davis, and, on behalf of the government, the Minister of Defence, Frederick Jones.

At the official welcome, Davis said: 'Jean, you are a very naughty girl, and really I think you want a good spanking for giving us such a terribly anxious time here . . .' Jones said the government might have liked to stop her taking the risk of crossing the Tasman, but 'being a woman I take it that our protests would only mean that she would be more determined to do the journey'.

This gaucheness was not peculiar to New Zealand. At a London luncheon in her honour, at the British Sportsmen's Club, the toast was to 'our little New Zealand lamb'. Such sentimental sexism was exacerbated by the fact that Batten looked gorgeous in an aviator's cap and goggles, and snared many a male admirer. No one seemed able to think of her as anything but girly, even though this first long-distance solo flight of 23,000 kilometres from England to New Zealand in eleven days and forty-five minutes, elapsed time, was a record that stood for forty-four years.

The greatest woman aviator in the pre-war pioneering decade of long-distance flying was born Jane Gardner Batten in Rotorua in 1909, the daughter of a strong-minded mother and a dentist father, whose marriage broke up in 1920. She was always called Jean. Her life seemed an inexorable progression from childhood to aviation fame, a climax from which she never recovered. Her mother, Ellen, pinned alongside her cot a picture of Louis Bleriot, the French aviation pioneer who had flown the English Channel not long before she was born. The family moved to Auckland when she was four and her mother took her to Mission Bay where the first New Zealander to achieve controlled, powered flight, Vivian Walsh, and his brother, Leo, were using flying-boats to train pilots for the First World War. During a 1929 visit to Sydney, her pushy mother arranged for Jean to fly with Charles Kingsford Smith, the man who had pioneered trans-Pacific and trans-Tasman flight. Mrs Batten was not so much hung up on her daughter being an aviator as succeeding in any career by breaking free from the constraints on women at that time. In childhood, Jean was to be a concert pianist, a performer of some kind. But the early interest in aviation turned into an obsession.

In 1930, mother and daughter went to London where Jean gained a flying licence and immediately set about planning a flight from England to Australia to break the women's record for the journey set that year by Englishwoman Amy Johnson. Money was the hurdle, though, so she returned to New Zealand in an unsuccessful search for sponsorship. Back in London, she borrowed money from two men who had fallen in love with her and made two attempts at the journey in 1933 and 1934, once crash-landing near Karachi and wrecking her de Havilland Gypsy Moth, and the second time running out of fuel near Rome and damaging the wings of another Gypsy Moth. Batten returned to London, borrowed wings from another aircraft and, two days after her arrival, set off again. This time she reached Darwin in just under fifteen days, breaking Johnson's solo record by four days, and becoming a famous international figure. Wildly celebrated in Australia and New Zealand, she turned her Gypsy Moth around and flew it back to London where she was also lionised.

Her next flight, in 1935, was a brilliant navigational feat, achieved in a new cabin aircraft, a Percival Gull 6. She was the first woman to fly from England to South

America – 8000 kilometres in sixty-one hours, fifteen minutes, elapsed time, a world record for any type of aircraft. Her leg across the South Atlantic, from Africa to Brazil, was also the fastest for any type of aircraft – sixteen hours, fifteen minutes. Her records were helped by the astonishing accuracy of her navigation, achieved with only a compass and a watch. No woman pilot had accomplished anything comparable. She was fêted around the world, revelled in her fame, and proved an able and entertaining speaker. She won the Harmon International Trophy for the most outstanding flight by a woman that year (jointly with Amelia Earhart), and again in 1936, when she was also awarded the CBE, and yet again in 1937. Although she was an outgoing and able speaker and seemed to enjoy the adulation, from time to time her mother and she fled to seclusion, often for months at a time.

After her record pioneering flight to New Zealand in 1936, followed by a demanding lecture tour, she recuperated from nervous exhaustion at Franz Josef in the South Island. Then she went to Sydney to be with Beverley Shepherd, an Australian airline pilot, the man she planned to marry. He died in an aircraft accident the day she arrived. She was grief-stricken and, with her mother, stayed incognito in Sydney for several months. Later in 1937, she flew her Percival Gull back to England in five days, eighteen hours, the fastest the route had ever been flown. She now held the solo record between the two countries in both directions.

This was the pinnacle of her career, from which her life went into a tailspin. When the Second World War arrived, she offered her services as a pilot, but only if she could fly her own aircraft. The government had no task for her in the Gull but confiscated it for the war effort. She did not offer to fly with the Air Transport Auxiliary delivering new aircraft, a role in which Amy Johnson was killed. She spent the war driving ambulances and working in a munitions factory. Although she was only thirty-six when the war ended she never flew an aircraft again.

In her unpublished memoir, she said she fell in love during the war with an RAF bomber pilot who was killed in action, another grievous emotional blow. Her disappointments in love were sad, but it is true that she had unofficially engaged to be married several times and had ruthlessly used men who fell for her to further her career. Since her childhood, her mother, Ellen, had provided her main emotional underpinning. They had always been close. From the time she retired from flying, they spent most of their time together and the relationship became unhealthy and reclusive. She had long before lost contact with her two brothers.

After the war Jean and her mother moved to Jamaica for a few years, living quietly and making few friends. Then they embarked on a peripatetic life, moving around Europe by car for nearly seven years before settling down again, this time in a small Spanish fishing village. During a holiday in Tenerife in 1966, Ellen, now eighty-nine, died. Jean was prostrate with grief for three years. She was alone. She and her mother had long ago shed their relationships with family and friends. Then, at age sixty, she had a facelift, dyed her hair black, donned miniskirts and travelled to England and New Zealand, her hand cupped to her ear, listening for echoes of her past fame and adulation. But few people remembered her name.

It was 1977 when she was in New Zealand and the newspapers splashed the story of her past but wrote more about her trimness and physical fitness. Her flying feats seemed brief and long ago, but the Prime Minister, Robert Muldoon, arranged for a state pension, not knowing that she had assets worth $100,000.

She spent the next few years living in Tenerife but travelled widely before moving to Majorca in 1982, where, only a month later, she died from blood poisoning, following a dog bite. She was alone when she died, unknown and unmourned in the town where she had intended to live out the rest of her life. She was buried in a pauper's grave. It was five years before her fate became known, thanks to the research of her biographer, Ian Mackersey, who called his book, *The Garbo of the Skies*. Her ending was sad and inglorious for a pretty and superbly talented, if ruthless and self-obsessed, woman who, for a brief five years, was queen of the air.

Forty-one

FIGHTING SANTA CLAUS

Political superstar of the 1930s, John A Lee was a team player – but only if he could be captain. And the only way he could be a captain was to lead a rebellion against the leadership of the first Labour government and take control of policy. He tried. He failed. In doing so, he became the villain of a piece of political theatre that ended the hopes of the extreme left and ensured New Zealand governments would remain pragmatic and centrist.

Lee's expulsion from the Labour Party at its annual conference in 1941 was the most sensational political event in the fourteen-year life of the first Labour government. He was admired for his bold and declarative oratory, his broadcasting skills, and for his pungent pamphleteering – talents that made him a powerful presence in the Labour Party and the House of Representatives and which had won him re-election for his Grey Lynn electorate in 1938 with the largest majority in New Zealand parliamentary history. But in the caucus of the Parliamentary Labour Party he was engaged in a struggle against the financial orthodoxy of Labour's leadership triumvirate: Prime Minister Michael Joseph Savage, his deputy Peter Fraser and the Minister of Finance, Walter Nash. Savage distrusted Lee, was perhaps jealous of his commanding populist skills, and had control over who was in Cabinet.

Lee's problem was that although he was admired, Savage was loved – an avuncular figure, in his time the most revered man in New Zealand political history, and it was his calmness and moderation the majority of voters liked most. As one journalist said later, attacking Michael Joseph Savage was like fighting Santa Claus.

John Alfred Alexander Lee was born in Dunedin in 1891, the son of Mary Isabella Taylor and Alfred Lee, a man with Romany blood, an entertainer and gymnast. The couple split when John was still a child. He worked in a boot shop and a printing factory but was twice convicted for theft, called 'incorrigible' by a magistrate and sentenced to Burnham Industrial School when he was fifteen. He escaped and was a fugitive for a few years, working in the country and carrying a swag among men he later helped immortalise in books such as *Shining with the Shiner*, *Shiner Slattery* and *Roughnecks, Rolling Stones and Rouseabouts*. But he had not mended his ways by 1911 when, as 'Alexander Leigh', he was convicted of smuggling liquor into the dry King Country and for breaking and entering. He spent a year in jail at Mt Eden. He served in the New Zealand Expeditionary Force in France during the First World War, was awarded the Distinguished Conduct Medal for bravery in 1917, was wounded in 1918 and had part of his left arm amputated.

In his teens, Lee read *The Jungle*, a novel about the unscrupulous capitalism of the US meat-packing industry by socialist writer Upton Sinclair, which made an impression on him, and triggered an interest in politics. As the years went by, he continued to read left-wing literature and to write socialist articles and pamphlets. Politics became an obsession and he began to understand that he had a quick brain, a ready pen and a powerful speaking voice. Even as an old man, the slim, straight-backed, brushy-haired, energetic Lee bounced his stentorian voice off the back of a cavernous hall where others needed a sound system.

On his return to New Zealand from the war, he quickly became a power in the Labour Party and the Returned Soldiers' Association and, when the party won the 1935 election with a landslide, he expected to become a Cabinet Minister. Savage, however, left him out but was persuaded to make him Under-Secretary for Housing. Lee launched and successfully developed the extraordinary state-housing programme. He was writing prolifically for political ends and also found time to write his first novel, *Children of the Poor*, which attracted critical attention in Britain and America. It was published anonymously at first, but his identity soon became known. Because it was largely autobiographical and portrayed his sister as a prostitute, the novel brought him odium from his political opponents and dismayed some of his associates. His claim was that the extreme poverty in which he grew up fostered crime.

Lee's egotism ballooned with success, and frustration

as Savage's refusal to give him full Cabinet responsibility pushed him to lead a left-wing rebellion against the political caution of Savage, Fraser and especially the financial orthodoxy of Nash. He wanted the Bank of New Zealand nationalised immediately, and fought Savage and Nash in caucus over pension and welfare amounts, the price the government paid for Reserve Bank shares when it was nationalised, the rate of interest offered in reconversion loan issues, the guaranteed prices for dairy products, and other issues. He wanted faster and more complete socialism.

Nash, though, had reason to be wary of repercussions. When the government gained power in 1935 with a programme of radical social reform, capital drained from the country, forcing him to impose exchange controls and go to London to arrange a loan. He found no takers until the Governor of the Bank of England, Montagu Norman, relented. It was a near thing and the message the Labour leadership got was not to stray too far from economic orthodoxy.

Lee was spokesman for a strong left-wing minority in caucus but could make no serious impression on policy and no advancement within the government. He was impatient. He wrote a letter to caucus members, attacking the party leadership, and especially Nash's financial policy, and had it published and widely distributed. As a result he was censured at the 1939 annual conference of the party, and a vote of confidence backed Nash. Then, after the Second World War broke out, it became known that Savage was seriously ill with cancer, and Lee was increasingly seen as divisive at a time when the government needed to demonstrate unity. Certain of his own rightness, his ego unbounded, he wrote an article called 'Psycho-Pathology in Politics' for the left-wing magazine *Tomorrow*. The article did not mention Savage by name but no one had any doubt at whom the attack was aimed. One passage read: 'An odd politician becomes physically, becomes mentally sick, and while he is physically and mentally sick, sycophants pour flattery on him. Like a child he will only play if he gets his way, he stays in the sickroom as a way of escape from problems. He becomes vain of mind and short of temper and believes that everybody who crosses his path has demoniac attributes . . .'

He ended the article with: 'There is no instance yet recorded in history of a party winning a people by carrying a leader on a sick-bed in front, by asking tomorrow to grow reverent at the odour of iodine.'

This character assassination of a dying man played into the hands of the right wing of the Labour Party. The article gave its leaders their chance to get rid of the socialist firebrand who was splitting the party nationally. Even some of Lee's left-wing associates winced at the clumsy, hurtful nature of the attack. He had been ordered by the national executive not to write for public consumption without approval. He refused to accept the censorship and wrote the offending *Tomorrow* piece. He was expelled from the party by 546 votes to 344 at the 1941 annual conference, despite a masterly speech in his own defence in which he said he could not endorse the 'Führerism within the Labour Party'.

As journalist Les Hobbs wrote some years later: 'And so when the final decision to expel Lee was taken, the atmosphere at the Labour conference . . . was as stickily sentimental as a television serial. The delegates . . . knew that while they talked, Savage, the man who had led them to victory and won for them both power and respectability, was near death. Lee never had a hope, especially when his article from *Tomorrow* was circulated and quoted at the conference.'

Two days after Lee was expelled, with the conference still in session, Savage died and the public left no doubt where its sentiments lay. The funeral cortège moved slowly by train from Wellington to Auckland, stopping at stations along the way to allow the people to express their grief. In Auckland, he was buried on the hill above Bastion Point in the last great memorial to a New Zealand politician.

The public had wanted economic security after the long trauma of the Depression. Although many Labour Party members were avowed socialists, most New Zealanders would have baulked at the reconstruction of the whole economy and the monetary system, even in the unlikely event that such policies could have succeeded in the face of opposition from the powerful nations with which a small trading nation had to do business. Lee was an immensely able, self-educated man but he was a maverick, one who, had he won the leadership, would almost certainly not have had the patience nor the humility required to head a parliamentary team for long.

After his expulsion, he languished in Parliament, formed the Democratic Labour Party but lost his seat at the next election, in 1943. He started *John A Lee's Weekly* and wrote novels and memoirs, relentlessly attacked the Catholic Church (to which Savage returned in his last months after being an atheist for most of his life), claiming it supported fascism. He later accused the unions and the Labour Party of subverting socialism and, as he grew older, surprised many people with his evolving political opinions, championing the American intervention in Vietnam and expressing his admiration for Prime Minister Robert Muldoon. He continued writing, and some of his political memoirs have been amusing and helpful to historians. He remained unrepentant, even after he had gained a measure of acceptance in his old age. He became a popular speaker during the 1960s and 1970s and was awarded an honorary LLD by the University of Otago in 1969. He died in 1982.

Footnote: Peter Fraser, who succeeded Savage as Prime Minister, established a reputation as an outstanding administrator, one of the most efficient leaders New Zealand has had. But the corruptions of power crept into his own soul. Within a few weeks of Lee's expulsion, *Tomorrow* was quietly destroyed. A policeman visited the head of the company that printed it. The man was told that he was responsible for the work produced in the factory and could face prosecution under wartime regulations. Fraser, the explosive radical who had gone to prison during the First World War for protesting against wartime conscription, lost office in 1949 after going on the stump around the country in favour of conscription in the strange peacetime of the Cold War.

Forty-two

DEATH-WISH PRISONERS
AND UNTRAINED GUARDS

The prisoner-of-war camp was still under construction as the Japanese prisoners began to arrive in 1942. The twenty-four-hectare site near Featherston, at the foot of the Rimutakas in the Wairarapa, had been an army training camp during the First World War. It was chosen as a prison site by Cabinet early in September, and the first 450 Japanese arrived before the end of that month.

A barbed-wire fence was stretched around the immediate area designed to hold the first prisoners, and two outer rows of coiled barbed wire were added later as a further deterrent to escape. Some few buildings, including primitive ablutions blocks, remained from the camp's previous existence. New huts were being built but most of the guards and the prisoners were initially housed in tents.

It was the first POW camp in New Zealand history, and even by this time Australia had few if any Japanese prisoners. The guards – 122 of them by the time the 1943 revolt erupted – were assembled quickly from among those rejected for medical or other reasons from fighting overseas or from among eighteen- and nineteen-year-olds waiting to come of age for overseas service. None of them or their officers had any experience or training in minding prisoners, mainly because no training was available. The prisoners had no idea of the provisions of the Geneva Convention which Japan had never ratified and no copies of the convention were available to them in Japanese.

The first few hundred prisoners were labourers and artisans captured by American forces on Guadalcanal and Tulagi, in the Solomons, where they had been engaged in such chores as airfield construction and maintenance, and the building of other facilities. They were tractable men who gave no trouble. The guards called them 'the workers'.

In the few weeks before Christmas, combatants began to arrive. They were mostly from the navy, many of them taken after the cruiser *Furutaka* was sunk off Guadalcanal. The two senior Japanese officers in the camp were off the *Furutaka*: Senior Lieutenant Kamikubo Sakujiro and Junior Lieutenant Adachi Toshio.

By February 1943, the still unfinished camp housed about 800 prisoners. The labourers, in Compound One, continued to work outside the camp, cutting scrub and gorse, but the combatants in Compound Two began to resist the demands that large parties of them should be required to report daily for work, which some regarded as aiding and abetting the enemy.

Japanese combatants were conventionally said to be wracked by self-hatred because they had allowed themselves to be captured whereas the emperor demanded of them that they should fight to the death or commit suicide, according to what was called the Bushido Code. Such was the shame of being captured that, according to one claim, some changed their names so they would be posted in Japan as missing rather than captured. None ever wrote letters home. Their attitude towards the guards was arrogant and often truculent and they pushed the warders as far as they could. Any problems between captors and captives were certainly exacerbated by the language and cultural chasm – by the Japanese sense of superiority over their ill-assorted guards, and by echoes of the fear New Zealanders had had for nearly a century of being swamped by Asian hordes. If Hitler wanted lebensraum for Germans in Europe, perhaps Asians sought expansion room even more. It was much easier for the Australian and New Zealand governments to demonise the Japanese than the Germans, who at least had Western cultural commonalities.

The popular and repeated account of what happened said that on the morning of 25 February a Japanese working party from Compound Two did not parade as ordered. A naval petty officer called Miyazaki refused a further order to parade a working party and after ten minutes of obduracy was taken forcibly from the compound. The other 295 in Compound Two also refused to parade and sat on the ground.

By 9.25 a.m., thirty armed guards, led by Lieutenant Malcolm, the adjutant, were inside the compound, covering the prisoners on three sides from between ten and fifteen metres. Guards were also stationed on the roofs of nearby buildings, one with a machine-gun. Two Japanese officers, who should not have been in Compound Two, Junior Lieutenant Adachi Toshio and Lieutenant Ikunosuke Nishimura, took control, speaking to the men and seeming to advise them to continue opposing the order to parade for work. They demanded to see the Commandant, Colonel Donald Donaldson, who was in his office. When advised of their demand, he simply told Malcolm that the rules must be obeyed and confirmed that force should be used if necessary. Donaldson stayed away from the compound until he heard the shooting start.

Guards forced their way through the shouting, defiant prisoners, with bayonets fixed, and arrested Nishimura. One Japanese was wounded in the thigh. Unarmed guards then tried to arrest Adachi but were beaten back by punching and kicking inmates. Adachi moved to the middle of the mob. Lieutenant Malcolm borrowed a revolver, ordered Adachi to come forward and fired a warning shot over his head when he refused. After a second command to Adachi to present himself was ignored, Malcolm fired at him, wounding him in the left arm.

The prisoners in Compound Two leapt to their feet and rushed forward, shouting as they went, hurling stones and wielding knives. The guards opened fire with rifles and tommy-guns from a concrete apron directly in front of the charging prisoners and from the top of the adjacent buildings. According to the official report, the ceasefire was given after less than a minute and the firing stopped. Forty prisoners lay dead and sixty-nine wounded. Eight of the wounded later died. More than a third of all the prisoners in the compound were hit. The wounded, including Adachi, were taken to hospitals in Featherston, Greytown, Masterton and Wellington. Seven guards were wounded, one fatally, from bullets that ricocheted from the concrete.

A representative of the International Red Cross visited the camp immediately afterwards and, because no chance of secrecy was possible, Prime Minister Peter Fraser publicly announced a few days later that the unfortunate incident was regretted but that 'firm action on the part of the guards was necessary to quell the riot and restore order' – which rather pre-empted the Court of Inquiry led by Colonel Guy Powles. The inquiry found resolute action had been needed and the shooting necessary for the protection of the guards and the people of the district. No one in the camp administration was found to be at fault, but the report did not condemn Adachi or Nishimura as culpable. It was ruled that the improvised weapons some of the prisoners had used proved the mutiny was premeditated.

The report had the tidy, wrapped-up feel of a wartime country that would have brooked no suggestion that the Japanese, demonised by propaganda, had any rights or that its own guards or officers had made any serious errors of judgement. For years, regular newspaper features appeared on what was called a 'riot' but was much more serious than that. The stories all had the same feel of bureaucratic substance. Those who suspected that the truth lay in the shadows had to wait more than forty years for light to be cast by Vincent O'Sullivan's play, *Shuriken*, and Mike Nikolaidi's formidably detailed and sensitive book, *The Featherston Chronicles*.

Why Donaldson, described as a stickler for discipline, did not go to the site and take control when the obduracy of the Japanese prisoners became pronounced is hard to understand. Two translators were available and perhaps a longer and calmer attempt should have been made to answer the Japanese complaints at the nature of the work they were being told to do and the large number of men required each day for working parties. Discrepancies remain between the official account and that of some eye-witnesses on such questions as who fired the first shot, how long the firing went on and whether shots were fired after a ceasefire order had been given. In a civilian context, answers to all the vexed questions associated with the shooting would have been sought and, while incidents were still fresh in participants' minds, may have been found; but in wartime, expedient answers were required.

However, Japanese officers themselves conceded later that a large number of the prisoners among the combatants were looking for some time and place to die. Given this, little doubt remains that some fatal confrontation was certain between the prisoners and their guards at Featherston, although no more real trouble was encountered at the camp, which remained until the repatriation of the remaining prisoners at the end of the war.

Some of the prisoners returned to Featherston for visits after the war, including Adachi, who was quoted by one source as saying in Wellington Public Hospital, immediately after the brief battle: 'I am sorry for the trouble I caused.'

Several attempts were made over many years to establish a peace garden on the site of the Featherston camp, but the local authorities and the Returned Servicemen's Association opposed it – unlike in Australia where an

even larger scale break-out occurred and left a higher
death toll on both sides.

Footnote: In 1944, a mass break-out by Japanese inmates
occurred from a POW camp in Cowra, in central New
South Wales. The camp held both Italian and Japanese
prisoners in separate compounds. A bugle sounded in the
Japanese barracks at 2 a.m. on 5 August and about 900
prisoners set fire to their huts and charged the fences,
using blankets and baseball gloves to get over the barbed
wire. Many of those unable to take part either killed
themselves or were murdered by others. More than a third
of them breached the outer perimeter but all were either
retaken or died by their own hand over the following ten
days. Two hundred and thirty-one of the prisoners were
killed and 108 wounded. Four Australians were killed in
the break-out; two of them were posthumously awarded
the George Cross for staying at their post manning a
Vickers machine-gun until they were overwhelmed by
escapers armed with knives and baseball bats.

Soon after the escape, a local woman, Mrs Weir,
refused to hand over two Japanese until she had given
them tea and scones as they had not eaten for days. The
two men returned to the Weir farm in the 1980s to thank
the family for their compassion.

A Japanese Garden and Cultural Centre was set up
in 1978, with Japanese government help, to honour the
dead on both sides.

Forty-three

THE PRICE WAR THAT SHOOK
A GOVERNMENT

The West Coast is a wild place, hemmed in on one side by the Southern Alps and on the other by a coast made doubly dangerous for shipping by heavy surf rolling in from the Tasman Sea and by a littoral drift that heaps treacherous bars across the entrances to all the harbours. And the prevailing westerly wind drops its rain in torrents to avoid heaving it over the alps.

Before good roads went through and before air services became regular, Coasters did not come and go much and in their isolation organised their own lives with contemptuous disregard for edicts from Wellington, or anywhere else for that matter. They were a tightly knit group of people – many of them miners who once panned and dug for gold, and later went into the pits for coal. Anywhere else in New Zealand you would be banned from amateur rugby if you played even one game of professional rugby league but on the Coast young men played rugby on Saturdays and league on Sundays, confident the New

Zealand Rugby Union knew that, should they ban anyone from rugby for playing league, Coasters would boycott the other game throughout the province.

In other parts of the country, hotel bars closed at 6 p.m. and stayed closed on Sundays, but Coasters tended to ignore licensing laws. The six o'clock swill never caught on because they liked beer inordinately and decided to drink it when it suited them best. After church or a league match on a Sunday was a good time.

Miners, by the nature of their dangerous business, stuck together like coal dust to a wet blanket, more cohesive even than other Coasters. When the first Labour government made trade unionism compulsory, these men revelled in a new, expanded, powerful form of mateship.

So it was that early in October 1947, when publicans decided to put the price of a ten-ounce beer up from sixpence to sevenpence, the Coast miners voted to boycott the pubs that charged the extra penny and, with the collective mateship that governed their lives, ruled that any renegade who paid sevenpence for a beer would be expelled from the union (and thus from his job). Five unionists were caught while the boycott lasted and it cost them their livelihood. A small matter this boycott, it may seem now, but it swelled into a confrontation that reached Cabinet.

The price of beer was controlled by an institution called the Price Tribunal, which was under the surveillance of the Minister of Industries and Commerce, Arnold Nordmeyer, a prim man with a squeaky voice he had once exercised from the pulpit as a Presbyterian minister. He pointed out that publicans could have cranked the price up to sevenpence eight years before, and in fact it had gone up in most of the rest of the country: it had been years before West Coast publicans could stiffen their resolve to make a move. Nordmeyer was too circumspect, though, to take sides.

The *Greymouth Star* pointed out that the price of travel on the government-owned railways, and the cost of essential commodities, including food, had gone up without the miners murmuring, let alone yelling, about government policies that caused the rises.

One heroic publican in Greymouth decided to continue to sell beer at sixpence a glass. He did brisk business from miners who spilled onto the streets from his premises as they crowded around to drink his beer.

The issue loomed large locally. The proprietor of the Railway Hotel in Hokitika challenged the secretary of the West Coast Trades Council to a public debate. A fight broke out in a pub at Kumara Junction, where Richard Seddon had been a publican sixty or more years before. A group of miners ordered beers and then refused to pay more than sixpence. The *Grey River Argus* reported soberly that, as a result, 'a fracas is alleged to have started. It is stated that the men grew restless and that glasses were smashed in the course of the disturbance, and it is reported that at least one man was hit over the head with a beer bottle.' The police were investigating, the report said.

The Westland Engine Drivers' Union joined the boycott, declaring seven-penny beers black.

Government politicians wanted nothing to do with the argument. A by-election campaign was under way and the Labour candidate tried a sidestep with: 'I'm afraid, as it is not a political question, I have not studied it.' If it wasn't then, it soon became a national political problem. A brewery in Dunedin was supplying that one pub in Greymouth still selling beer for sixpence. The publican's organisation, the Licensed Victuallers' Association, suggested the brewery cease deliveries to the renegade publican. The miners told the New Zealand Transport Workers' Union in Wellington, which told the government, that if the beer didn't get through, beer deliveries would be declared black nationally. Guess what? The beer got through.

A month after the boycott began, eighteen unions on the Coast had joined the campaign against sevenpenny beers. One of the men who was sent to Coventry for paying the new price was a J O'Leary, who said in a letter to the *Greymouth Star* that he had been one of those who had left the country to fight in defence of liberty – which was a roundhouse swing at his fellow miners, who had been protected against conscription during the war because they worked in an essential, protected industry. Defiantly, he condemned the union as a dictatorship.

In the meantime, the miners had bought two houses in Greymouth and began the work of joining them together as premises for a working-men's club. They had no doubt they would get a club licence from an increasingly rattled government. By Christmas, new working-men's clubs had also opened in Brunner and Runanga. No club licences had been issued in New Zealand for fifty years, but the government decided to include provisions for chartered club licences in the 1948 revision of licensing legislation.

So after a year of operating illegally, in typical disregard for what was going on in the rest of the country,

'Workingmen's Clubs and Mutual Schools of Art' were chartered on the West Coast and formally made legal. The 'art' referred to in the clubs' names was a typical local joke. The art, they claimed, was in the drinking.

The boycott lasted until February 1948, when the Licensed Victuallers' Association gave its publican members the option of reverting to sixpenny beers, which they did – but, some say, in slightly smaller glasses. By then, the working men had their clubs open and trading briskly.

The militant unionists at that time shared a camaraderie that few groups have ever done in New Zealand history, and most often, with memories of the Depression still fresh in their minds, they used their power to better themselves and other workers. But like all power it ultimately corrupted. Apart from depriving dissenters of their jobs, the miners decided at the end of their campaign to boycott the publican who had continued to serve them sixpenny beers when all the others refused to do so.

Why? Because he had scabbed on his mates in the Licensed Victuallers' Association.

Forty-four

POLSON'S POSSE BECOMES
A SUICIDE SQUAD

In they filed, the twenty-six new Members of the Legislative Council, led by seventy-five-year-old political warhorse William Polson intent on the mercy killing of the Legislative Council which had been formed by the British government ninety-eight years before. The council was moribund, anyway, and unlamented by anyone but those of its members who had snoozed there for years as the beneficiaries of political patronage.

It was August 1950, and Polson's posse was dubbed the 'suicide squad' because they had been appointed to the Legislative Council by Prime Minister Sidney Holland with the precise task of killing it by passing the Legislative Council Abolition Bill and sending it back to the House of Representatives. The squad did the deed expeditiously and New Zealand became the only single-chamber Parliament in the British Commonwealth, and one of the few in democracies around the world.

The new appointees replaced some retiring Labour

members and swelled the ranks from thirty-one to fifty-two. Polson was the man for the job of leader of the Council, ensuring no backsliders tried to commute the death penalty imposed by Holland. He had had a long career as a farmer and in farming politics, plus nearly twenty years as an MP, and had helped Holland win a leadership tussle soon after the National Party was formed. He had remained a confidant. As a young man he worked as a journalist for both Wellington's *Evening Post* and *The Press* in Christchurch, and later became involved in farming journalism. He was known for his no-nonsense, confrontational personality.

It all began back in 1852 when the Imperial government bestowed on New Zealand by Act of Parliament a measure of self-government through a Legislative Council and House of Representatives, although serious limitations on the power of Parliament remained with the Crown and its representative, the Governor. In fact, the Governor appointed Members of the Legislative Council (MLCs), and the remoteness of New Zealand at a time when transport and communications were primitive meant he had more real power and influence than his bosses in London. The MLCs were appointed by the Governors (Governors-General after 1917) for life in the spirit of the House of Lords, and their role was to provide a wise second look at legislation in the best interests of the nation, without having to worry about the political pressures of needing to be re-elected.

That was the theory, but in reality the Council was stacked with conservative members of the Establishment to the taste of the British aristocrats who were appointed Governors. By the time the House of Representatives settled on a two-party system in 1890, the radical Liberal Party was elected to power and its leader, John Ballance, wanted to pack the Council with new appointees to get the trail-blazing legislation through. In 1891, a seven-year term was imposed on new MLCs, which meant the membership could be increased without the total growing out of control. However, Lord Onslow and his successor Lord Glasgow resisted Ballance's request with the unblinking political partisanship of the class they represented. Ballance thought he would have to go back to the electorate but his growing popularity with the majority of New Zealanders – especially since he had turned down the blandishment of a knighthood – finally persuaded the Colonial Office in London to tell Glasgow to comply.

But this meant that each succeeding government used the Council membership to bestow a retirement benefit on its former MPs and other old retainers and supporters. It became something of an old man's home. In 1914, William Massey's Reform government passed legislation providing for a Council of forty members elected by proportional representation, along with three appointed Maori members. But, curiously, the Act was never implemented.

In 1947, the burgeoning National Party with energetic Opposition leader Sidney Holland introduced the Legislative Council Abolition Bill. The Labour government wasn't too enthusiastic about the Council either but many in the party, including its MLCs, could see the end of the golden perk. The Attorney-General suggested the Bill could cause legal problems unless New Zealand adopted the Statute of Westminster, British legislation enacted in 1931 offering constitutional independence to New Zealand, Australia, Canada, Newfoundland, South Africa and the Irish Free State. The countries had to adopt the statute. Most of the former colonies took their autonomy fairly quickly but Australia waited eleven years and New Zealand sixteen – and only then made its move for freedom because of this Legislative Council problem.

The National Party, in its pledges for the 1949 election, declared it would abolish the Council, but also promised alternative ways of saving the country from rapid and retrospective legislation. It honoured the first pledge but not the second. A Constitutional Reform Committee recommended in 1952 that a senate be set up with thirty-two members nominated by parties in proportion to their strength in the House of Representatives. The recommendation was ignored. Holland gave an undertaking that legislation would not be passed within a stipulated period of being introduced, but that was rapidly forgotten and New Zealand fell under the control of a majority of its Cabinet.

A petition to Parliament in 1960 sought both a written constitution and an upper house. After hearings, MPs from both main parties opposed any such changes. The matter was laid to rest for more than twenty years. Then legislation pushed through the House with extreme haste in the mid-1980s by the Labour government gave rise to more talk of a second chamber, and motivated many people to vote for the MMP system of proportional voting.

So big, blunt Bill Polson and his euthanasia troupe swelled the ranks of the Legislative Council in 1950 not to praise it but to bury it, before the National government had been in power for a year. The Council passed the Abolition Bill by a majority of ten votes, after some undignified speeches from those who opposed it and sought some form of compensation for loss of job. The measure passed through the House of Representatives with little resistance from Labour. The demise created a unicameral Parliament more than fifty years ago, and New Zealanders seem to have no vision of a second coming.

Forty-five

COLD WAR CONFRONTATION

A hot war was raging in Korea in 1951 when a Cold War stand-off came to New Zealand. On the left was the leader of the Waterside Workers' Union, Jock Barnes, who saw his role as leading the fight against fascism. On the right was Prime Minister Sid Holland, an avowed Cold War warrior against Communism. Barnes was a brilliant platform speaker who had ready access to his members in donkey-rooms throughout the country in which watersiders could be summoned at short notice to what they called stop-work meetings – meetings in the employers' time. I attended two of them as a 'seagull' (part-time watersider) and marvelled at his powerfully persuasive oratory of the sort you only ever hear now from cult leaders.

Holland was a quick-thinking, smart tactician with tight command over his party, a good sense of where middle New Zealand opinion lay, and a pronounced authoritarian streak.

It is not too much to say that New Zealand's political and economic future was shaped by the nature of the struggle that followed the Waterside Workers' Union's refusal to work overtime that February. The government decided to break the back of the militant unions.

The setting was this. When it came into power in 1950, the new National government had ended petrol and butter rationing, released land sales from control, allowed state-house tenants to buy their houses at low mortgage rates, and then ended food subsidies. Some other economic restrictions the Labour government had left in place at the end of the war were also loosened. Otherwise, the welfare state remained pretty well intact. National had even campaigned that its benefits system would be better than Labour's. But the sudden release of economic controls had triggered inflation and then the war in Korea created a bonanza market for wool, launching what was close to hyperinflation. The government intervened to delay wool income to farmers in a bid to arrest inflation, but merely reduced it a little.

New Zealand troops were, controversially, fighting in Korea at the time of the strike. Kay Force, as it was called, was an artillery regiment supported by transport services. Eventually 2000 men served as part of a Commonwealth Division.

The removal of food subsidies in particular and inflation in general set trade unions clamouring for increases in their wages, which were largely controlled. In July 1950, the hourly rate for watersiders had been increased to four shillings and threepence. In January 1951, the Court of Arbitration granted an increase of fifteen per cent to other workers. The watersiders' union immediately applied to have the fifteen per cent added to its members' wages, over and above their recent increase. The Port Employers' Association offered four shillings and sevenpence halfpenny an hour. The union replied with a demand for five shillings and twopence.

Neither side would budge.

On 13 February, the watersiders throughout the country started an overtime ban. They would work only forty hours a week, between 8 a.m. and 5 p.m. Their employers and the government decided that the wharves could not be worked under those conditions and, anyway, that this did not comply with their terms of employment.

Impasse.

The left wing of the trade-union movement had broken away from the more conservative Federation of Labour, headed by anti-communist stalwart Fintan Patrick Walsh. They had formed the Trades Union Council. Although the watersiders were joined in the strike by miners, seamen, freezing workers and some other unions, the indications early on were that the majority of the FOL unions would either stay out of the fight or back the government and employers.

The strikers should have known, too, that Holland was doggedly antagonistic towards militant unionism. In September 1942, at a low point for the Allies during the war, miners at Huntly went on strike. Ten miners claimed they could not make the minimum wage because their production levels were low as a result of rocks in the coalface. They wanted their pay topped up by nine shillings a day. Management claimed the men were on a go-slow, as other teams had kept production up on the same face only three weeks previously. All Waikato

collieries came out in sympathy, which meant that the
war effort lost about 15,000 tons of coal a week – just as
the NZEF Second Division was preparing for the Battle
of El Alamein. Many of the miners were not conscripted
into the armed forces because their job was classified
essential.

One hundred and eighty miners were charged with
being parties to an illegal strike and each was sentenced
to a month in prison. Then the government decided to
take control of the mine for the duration of the war,
the miners returned to work, and the sentences were
deferred. But resolution without punishment was not
good enough for Sid Holland. He led the five other
National Party members out of the wartime coalition
Cabinet on the grounds the ringleaders of the strike
should have been imprisoned and the rest of the strikers
given forty-eight hours to get back to work or be forced
into the army. Two of his colleagues, Gordon Coates and
Adam Hamilton, rejoined the war Cabinet when invited
on a personal basis, but Holland remained intractable in
the face of militant unionism.

And so it proved again in 1951. Once the watersiders
refused overtime in February, the Holland government
deregistered the union, shut them out of the wharves and
moved the armed forces in – mainly the army to work
the wharves, and navy and air force personnel to move
urgent supplies by sea and air. With some justification,
watersiders called it a lock-out, not a strike.

The strike became bitter as the watersiders and
their supporters realised that no general strike would
eventuate and the FOL unions were not about to join
them. Indeed, Walsh was outspoken in his opposition

to the strikers, openly accusing them of being under the control of Communists. Public opinion had been moving against union militancy for some time, and the Holland government knew that. However, many people who had little sympathy for the watersiders were appalled when the government declared a state of emergency under the Public Safety Conservation Act of 1932. Among other draconian measures, the union's money was impounded; it became a criminal offence to materially help a striker, to speak in public on the issue, to protest on behalf of the strike, or to conduct a public meeting. The government was entitled to intercept private correspondence.

The Labour Party Opposition, led by the equivocating Walter Nash, attempted to intercede to reach a compromise but the Holland government wanted to grasp the opportunity to break the left-wing unions once and for all. Holland announced, on 15 March, a platform on which a settlement could be reached. The seven points included a procedure for the swift investigation and settlement of waterside disputes; that ways be devised to speed up the turn-around of ships; that secret ballots should always be taken on strike issues; and that the union should not have control over who had permanent, full-time employment on the wharves.

The FOL unions accepted the conditions quickly and unanimously, and these included the seamen's union and those representing general workers and railway workers. Almost every union was back to work by early April.

The watersiders held out, but the government then began to recruit workers for new waterside workers' unions – not one embracing national body but one union in each of the ports. Despite violence as the striking workers tried to keep scab unions from forming, they were clearly fighting a rearguard action even though Barnes, who prided himself on being a battler, remained adamant the union would prevail.

The government had decided it would break the militants and emerge as the champion of law and order and anti-communism, and they succeeded, although it took them longer than they had expected. By mid-July, the emergency regulations had been withdrawn, and unionists – many of them from the former militant union – were back on the wharves but working under a vastly different, less preferential set of rules. The government passed the Industrial Conciliation and Arbitration Amendment Act, which ensured secret ballots on major union issues, redefined strikes, and kept unions local rather than national, thus diminishing their power. The government resisted calls for an end to compulsory unionism brought in by Labour in the 1930s on the grounds that with secret ballots unions would be more responsible and, if they were contained within groups, workers' demands could be more easily controlled.

But the menace to democracy, which revealed the despotic streak in the Holland administration, lay in the Police Offences Act passed in December 1951, which made picketing or protesting on behalf of illegal strikes a criminal offence, and included vague definitions of seditious intention and seditious literature that would be illegal if it endangered 'public safety'. These were redolent of Cold War panic in some other Western countries, and were repealed by the Labour government in 1959.

But in 1951, the Labour Party was in disarray. Despite

public distaste for the ruthlessness of the Holland government and its disregard for democratic rights, Labour was seen as inept, weakened by disunity and ineffective in the face of a crisis. During the Address-in-Reply debate, Nash moved a vote of no confidence in the government on the grounds of poor economic performance affecting the cost of living. It was a forlorn hope that anyone would take much notice of that, pertinent though it was, during and after such prolonged industrial chaos.

As the strike ended, Holland announced an abrupt dissolution of Parliament and a snap election for September. His confidence that public opinion was behind him was justified by the result which increased the government's majority from twelve to twenty seats. But a close look at the result reveals that both parties actually lost voter support compared with the previous election. Labour was down three and a third per cent and National half of one per cent. The overall voter turnout was down by nearly five per cent, suggesting that many who may have disapproved of the watersiders' action were also disillusioned by the behaviour of both political parties.

The crisis on the wharves had distracted the public from the inept economic performance of the inexperienced National government in the months after it came to power. But after the strike, the party held power until 1957 when Labour, led by the ageing and waffling Walter Nash, won a one-term tenure before a Keith Holyoake-led National government held power through the 1960s.

More than 20,000 workers took part in the 1951 strike with about 15,000 of them idle for almost all of the 151 days it lasted. The annual report of the Waterfront

Commission reported that watersiders lost more than £1.5 million in wages.

The unions, which had done so much to improve the quality of life in New Zealand through the 1930s and 1940s, were dominated for more than a decade by the conservative FOL leader Walsh, and were never again as strong after 1951.

Forty-six

STAND-OFF AT BASTION POINT

On a January morning in 1977, a group of people from the Orakei hapu of Ngati Whatua moved on to disputed land at Bastion Point, one of the loveliest sites around the perimeter of Waitemata Harbour. From the high grassy vantage, they could see Rangitoto, the last volcano to blow its top in the region, slumbering in the summer haze, almost full frame in the picture of the morning. A few years before, hotel magnate Sir Henry Kelliher had dreamt of building a five-star hotel somewhere on this matchless site. He got to the design stage but in the end could not get access to the land.

The small band of people who moved on to the site that day did not dispute that it was Crown land, but they were adamant that how it had changed hands over 160 years, from Ngati Whatua to the government, dishonoured a generous gift from their tribe. They called them-selves the Orakei Maori Action Group. They knew they were breaking the law by trespassing, and this had caused dissension within the hapu. But they stayed. And stayed. And after this Bastion Point conflict was finally resolved, no government dared to stare down Maori on any land question until it had been examined. The opposition of the action group proved too determined and, on examination, their case too just.

After a century of slumbering resentment, Maori awoke to the power of protest in the late 1960s. During that decade, women and indigenous people had forced governments in Western countries to attend to old injustices and inequalities. New Zealand was in the vanguard of the feminist struggle for equal power with men, and early in the 1970s, Maori clambered aboard the protest train. Many of them considered land ownership the issue that impinged most on their mana and their future economic prospects. They believed their own conventional institutions such as the New Zealand Maori Council and the Maori Women's Welfare League had not pursued forceful enough policies, had indeed been subsumed into the Establishment by various governments.

Early signs of Maori determination to adopt a more confrontational approach included the formation of Nga Tamatoa, a radical political organisation whose young membership included a clever and determined group of women. Maori had gained substantial Pakeha support as the government and the New Zealand Rugby Union resisted an international campaign to act against sporting contacts with South Africa. Eva Rickard's thirty-year fight to have land returned that had been confiscated for defence purposes during the Second World War ended when the wider public became aware that what had occurred was a blatant land steal.

Then came the seminal Maori Land March of 1975. This hikoi from Northland to Wellington, led by the indomitable Whina Cooper, attracted thousands of marchers. By then, political pressure on land grievances had built up to the point where the government established the Waitangi Tribunal to investigate claims. At the end of that year, a National government led by Robert Muldoon came to power and brought about an abrupt change of attitude. The government announced a plan to subdivide the last twenty-five hectares of uncommitted Crown land at Bastion Point for high-income housing and parks. Ngati Whatua had hoped to reclaim the land through the Waitangi Tribunal. Once in private ownership, the land would be forever beyond their reach.

So in January 1977, Orakei Maori Action Committee members, led by Joe Hawke, occupied the contested land, causing a split within the Orakei hapu. The protesters' action also had only limited support from the broader community, which knew little of the background to the Ngati Whatua claims.

In March 1840, the Orakei paramount chief, Te Kawau, accompanied by other hapu chiefs, went to the Bay of Islands, signed the Treaty of Waitangi and invited Governor Hobson to move to the Waitemata Harbour to share their land. Maori at the time were still attracted to European settlers for economic reasons, and Te Kawau was aware that an added attraction would be protection from other tribes, especially from the musket raiders in the north. Later that year, Hobson chose Auckland as his new capital and Ngati Whatua agreed to hand over more than 1200 hectares for the site of a town, with details of sale to be worked out later. The hapu gave land for a chapel and a school to the Anglican Church in 1858 and offered Takaparawha Point to the government for gun emplacements to resist a feared Russian invasion, a scare that lasted for more than thirty years. The offer was accepted, but the land was never used for that purpose and never given back.

Although the presence of the Europeans undoubtedly did give protection to local Maori in the early years, the Ngati Whatua returned the favour by helping guard the settlement against southern tribes in the 1860s. Ngati Whatua sold thousands of hectares of land as more settlers arrived, but Governor George Grey ruled that most of it should not have been sold privately according to the Treaty, bought much of it back, and confiscated some. The government paid the hapu £341 for the 1200 hectares originally given and six months later sold eighteen hectares on to settlers for £25,275. The sale money was used to build roads, bridges and other infrastructure for the fast-growing new town.

Te Kawau had made it clear the 285 hectares of tribal land at Orakei was not for sale and by 1854 that was the only land the hapu retained. In 1869, the Native Land Court gave the title of the land to thirteen claimants against the wishes of the hapu. In 1886, the government confiscated more than five hectares of the headland at Bastion Point for defence purposes under the Public Works Act, and paid £1500 in compensation when the hapu took a case to the Compensation Court, a grant absorbed by lawyers.

The government legislated to take land including the waterfront at Okahu Bay for the town's main sewer outfall, which began polluting the bay in 1914. The hapu began to break up as conditions became difficult on the ancestral settlement site. From that time on, the government and private buyers bought the land from owners who had been given the power by the courts to act independently of the hapu. In 1951, the government took the remaining five hectares from Ngati Whatua.

Against this historical backdrop, the government decided in 1976 to subdivide for private development the twenty-five hectares of former Ngati Whatua land not yet built on. The response of the Orakei Maori Action Committee was to fight for this last chance to regain some of the hapu land that had slipped away through the action of successive governments and a number of individuals the tribe considered to be unauthorised to sell by tradition and tribal lore.

The protesters stayed on Bastion Point for seventeen months. Then, on 25 May 1978, 500 policemen, backed by fifty vehicles, including thirty, three-tonne army trucks, encircled the 200 protesters and their ramshackle shelters. Once the police were in position, the Commissioner of Crown Lands in Auckland drove in on the back of an army vehicle and announced through a loudhailer that the protesters were on Crown land, and issued three warnings that they were trespassing and that those who stayed would be arrested.

He handed over to the Auckland chief of police, Assistant Commissioner JW Overton, who announced, 'This area will be cleared and we hope to accomplish this without force.' The protest remained passive as the occupants were taken away for formal charging, many of them tearful and singing lamentations. Their shelters were demolished by an army bulldozer.

The massive military nature of the operation against peaceful protesters alienated many ordinary citizens who may have felt support for the government until then; and in the long term the protesters triumphed. Later that year, largely in response to the protest, the Crown returned some land taken under the Public Works Act which had not been used for the designated purpose. But there was a charge – $200,000.

Six years later, a claim was lodged by Ngati Whatua with the Waitangi Tribunal that they had been wrongfully deprived of the 280-hectare Orakei block which ought to have been kept in tribal ownership for ever. On the recommendation of the tribunal the government returned part of the Orakei land – one parcel of which can never be sold or leased, and another that may be developed – and awarded Ngati Whatua $3 million to help with the development.

Okahu Park, with its popular city beachfront, was restored to tribal ownership, and is now managed jointly by the hapu and the Auckland City Council for the enjoyment of the whole Auckland community.

The Bastion Point conflict was a long-running news story which at first split the nation because of what even the Waitangi Tribunal condemned as an illegal occupation. But the combination of Ngati Whatua determination, government overreaction and the revelation that the Orakei hapu had been unjustly treated encouraged other Maori groups to assert their claims vigorously and the government to examine more intently those cases in which the guarantees of the Treaty of Waitangi had been unjustly swept aside.

North Island

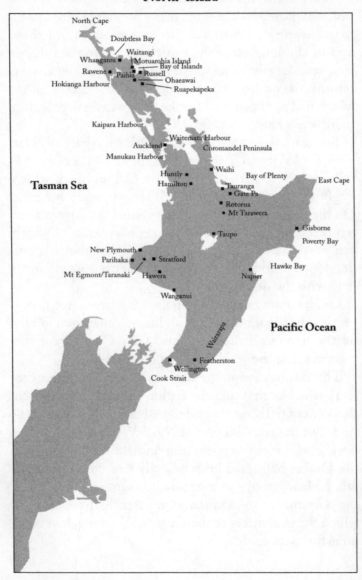

North Cape
Doubtless Bay
Waitangi
Whangaroa
Motuarohia Island
Bay of Islands
Rawene
Russell
Paihia
Ohaeawai
Hokianga Harbour
Ruapekapeka

Kaipara Harbour

Waitemata Harbour
Auckland
Coromandel Peninsula
Manukau Harbour

Tasman Sea

Waihi
Huntly
Bay of Plenty
East Cape
Hamilton
Tauranga
Gate Pa
Rotorua
Mt Tarawera

Gisborne
Taupo
Poverty Bay

New Plymouth
Parihaka
Stratford
Hawke Bay
Mt Egmont/Taranaki
Hawera
Napier

Wanganui

Waitrapa

Pacific Ocean

Featherston
Wellington
Cook Strait

South Island

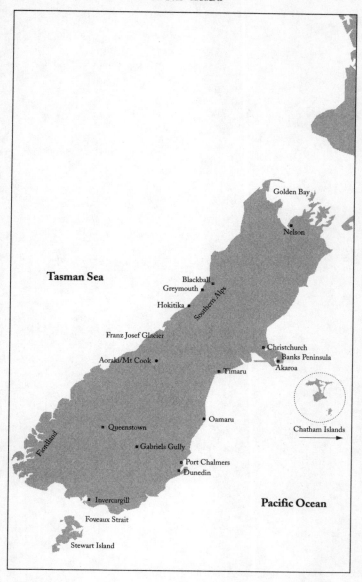

Tasman Sea

Golden Bay

Nelson

Blackball
Greymouth
Hokitika

Southern Alps

Franz Josef Glacier

Aoraki/Mt Cook

Christchurch
Banks Peninsula
Akaroa

Timaru

Chatham Islands

Oamaru

Fiordland

Queenstown

Gabriels Gully

Port Chalmers
Dunedin

Invercargill

Pacific Ocean

Foveaux Strait

Stewart Island